THE IMPRESSIONISTS

EDGAR HILAIRE GERMAIN DEGAS: PRIMA BALLERINA

THE IMPRESSIONISTS

Wilhelm Uhde

THE PHAIDON PRESS · VIENNA
OXFORD UNIVERSITY PRESS · NEW YORK

PRINTED IN GERMANY
PRINTED IN AUSTRIA
SECOND EDITION

PRINTED IN GERMANY
PRINTED IN AUSTRIA
SECOND EDITION

THE IMPRESSIONISTS
BY WILHELM UHDE

I.
ÉDOUARD MANET

Of Édouard Manet's personal appearance we know that he was of average height, that he wore a short, square beard, that he had fair hair and vivacious deep-set eyes. His manners were smooth and courteous, and he was always well dressed, in the fashion of his time.

As to the appearance of his pictures, we find the following description in an article written by Émile Zola in 1867: "His paintings are light-coloured and luminous, with a concrete and tangible pallor. The light in them is white and wide-spread, casting a gentle glow over the objects depicted."

His personal appearance and demeanour give scant indication of his human qualities, and in the same way the luminous aspect of his pictures is of little importance in determining their place in art. The latter seems to me to have been admirably defined by Paul Valéry—though it is true that he gives no grounds for his statement—in the following words: "The fame of Manet's name was assured by the quality of his admirers, and above all by their diversity. These devotees of his painting, differing so widely in character, united in asserting that his place was among the great masters, among those men whose art and authority have endowed the flowers of a day, the changing fashions, the bodies of human beings and the fleeting glances of their eyes with a kind of permanence which will endure for centuries, and a spiritual and interpretative value which may be compared with that of a sacred text."

After Manet's death Edgar Degas uttered the expressive words: "He was greater than we thought."

The above statements need explanation and substantiation, and this is possible only by means of a brief delineation of the history of his pictures, which forms a striking contrast to the banal and typical story of his everyday life. For this well-dressed, urbane man, with his check waistcoat and his tall hat, who spent his afternoons in the Café Tortoni, this sociable Parisian, very much the "galant homme" and something of a dandy, who glided noiselessly through a conventional world, seems to have led a double life. Side-by-side with the tranquil existence of a good bourgeois, respecting the petty formalities of his milieu and at the same time following the conventional path of a man of the world who had liaisons and fought duels, there existed the eventful life of an artist who seemed to be turning upside-down all the laws of painting. The former of these two existences seems to have had no other purpose than to give chronological order and dates to the latter; it seems to be nothing but a silken thread holding together a chain of beautiful pearls.

Of this thread there is little to be said except that it began at one point and ended at another, but we shall of necessity often be conscious of it when we come to examine any of those pearls whose beauty attracts us, and before which we pause longer than before the others which we allow to glide noiselessly through our fingers.

As we want to allow the external circumstances of Manet's life—as they have been described by Théodore Duret and others—to lead us to his various pictures, we will begin by recording that Édouard Manet was born on January 23rd, 1832, at 5 Rue Bonaparte, Paris, and baptized in the church of Saint-Germain-des-Prés. His father was a legal functionary, his mother's maiden name was Fournier, and both she and her husband came from well-to-do old middle-class families. Édouard studied at the Collège Rollin, where his teachers certified that his work was thoroughly unsatisfactory and his ideas confused. It would have been in accordance with family tradition if, after leaving school, he had devoted himself to the study of the law. The intention of becoming a painter, which he first expressed when he was sixteen, startled his family. A compromise was reached and he became a sailor, embarking for Rio de Janeiro on the "Havre et Guadeloupe". When asked to do so, he drew caricatures of the captain and officers. Soon the first opportunity of exercising his artistic talent came his way; the colour of a consignment of cheese had been ruined, and Édouard restored it to its original freshness by painting it over.

On his return he succeeded in getting his own way and in 1850 we find him studying at Couture's studio. Manet did not get on at all with his teacher, who has given us some charming small-size heads but otherwise created only stiff arrangements of the "Classical Ideal" with professional models. Couture uttered the ominous prophecy: "You will never be more than the Daumier of your time."

About 1856 Manet left this studio, and we can understand that for him it was not enough. From it he went to the Louvre, and then, following Couture's advice, abroad, to Holland, where Frans Hals interested him, to Dresden and Munich. He copied a Rembrandt and a Titian, admired the great Venetians in Italy, visited Florence and copied a head by Filippo Lippi. Then he returned to the Louvre, where he copied Titian's "Madonna with the rabbit", one of Tintoretto's self-portraits and the horsemen of Velázquez. Between 1851 and 1860 he also paid a visit to Delacroix, whose "Barque of Dante" he asked to be allowed to copy.

The Louvre was a school suited to his rank. There he found himself on an equal footing with kindred masters, he discovered the values which were suited to his talents, mastered them and thus collected the elements which go to form his greatness. These were based on his affection for the rare and supreme values to be found only in a few masters, in Titian, Velázquez, Rembrandt and one or two others, to whom Valéry's words are applicable, that they endowed the flowers of a day with a permanence which will endure for centuries and made of them sacred texts.

An attempt to determine Manet's position by an analysis of the purely artistic values in his pictures —in this case we are concerned chiefly with the works of his early period—is particularly difficult because the material available is not sufficient to enable us to form a judgement as to the highest values. The plastic values, by which we mean the expressive and tactile values, those of movement and space, and lastly of composition, have nothing to do with the determining of Manet's place in art, for they can scarcely give rise to disagreement. The position to be assigned to Manet depends entirely on the purely artistic values. Among these colouring and colour-harmonies, which are of great beauty in his works, constitute the least important category, for nowadays they can be assessed by standards comprehensible to all. The two higher categories of artistic values, to be found in the works of great masters and therefore also in those of Manet, have hitherto scarcely been established as phenomena, let alone been given a terminology. In the case of one of the two, the use of grey, which holds an almost supreme position in painting, not as a colour to be arranged with the other colours but with pretensions to individual beauty, the best term one can use is perhaps "value of grey tones". The frequency with which such tones occur in Manet's works raises them to a higher level than, for instance, those of Van Gogh. But his real place is determined by the values which ensue when the grey tone values are brought into contact with other colour values which are suited to them, without being blended to form harmonies, and which have sufficient character to retain their independence. In such cases of artistic polyphony, it is best to speak of "melodic values".

Several years were to pass before Manet's hand gave birth to a "sacred text" which it will be our task to consider and interpret. For his experiences in the Louvre still dominated his mind and he could not free himself from them in a day. Nevertheless in many of his pictures from this period we can detect elements, from the totality of which the high quality of his personality was to emerge. He painted a portrait of Antonin Proust, whom he had known as a child at the Collège Rollin and afterwards at Couture's studio, the same who subsequently, as Minister of Fine Arts, often gave him friendly assistance. He also painted the "Absinthe-Drinker", on seeing which Couture exclaimed: "There is only one absinthe-drinker, and that's the man who painted this idiotic picture." He painted the "Child with the cherries" and the "Concert in the Tuileries Gardens", one of the most precious documents we possess concerning the Second Empire, in which he himself, Baudelaire and Théophile Gautier all figure. He painted the portrait of his parents, in which some have seen the influence of Frans Hals, a picture in which the dominating element of the grey tone already makes a victorious appearance. In 1861 he painted the "Child with a sword" and in the following year the "Vagrant Musicians", before which we used to sit so often before the war, to drink in its exhilarating and at the same time tranquillizing browns, just as we used to go sometimes to the Gallimard Collection to enjoy the grey of a little still-life of oysters which he painted one year before. Grey now begins to appear in many variations in his pictures, from the stately dark tone to the grey in his "Street Singer", which Zola called "soft and blond". From now on this "blond" grey of Manet's will take its place beside the luminous grey of Titian, the severe Spanish grey of Ribera, the aristocratic grey of Velázquez, and the many others characteristic of Guardi, Lenain, Chardin and Corot. An essential element of his art was thus added to the others, and several pictures of this period, such as the portrait of Victorine Meurend and the "Young man with a dog", already display in a perfect form the pure artistic physiognomy of Manet and the full beauty of his work.

Wandering troupes of Spanish singers and dancers provided him with models for pictures in Spanish costumes. He felt more and more kinship with Velázquez, El Greco and Goya. He painted a Spanish ballet, a matador saluting the crowd, a young woman in toreador costume, a young man dressed as Majo, the guitarrist, which brought him an honourable mention from the committee of the Salon. All these he painted, and they form a kind of halo round that priceless and decisive work, the first by his hand which may be regarded and interpreted as a "sacred text": the "Lola de Valence".

Let us consider this picture as we now see it in the Camondo Collection at the Louvre. Originally it had a neutral background. Manet added the background of dark theatrical scenery later. But it is this background, in its relationship to the rest, which heightens the quality of the picture, which gives it an additional value, difficult to achieve and seldom realized, to be found only in the works of the greatest masters. In order to understand in what this value consists, let us compare the picture with two others which hang close-by. One is a stable scene with horses fighting, by Delacroix, the other is Corot's celebrated picture of a studio. Two different kinds of artistic values are realized in these. In the Delacroix we find firm colour values of green, reddish-brown and grey-white which blend together to form a complete harmonic value. In the Corot there is an abundance of grey tones, of regal descent, for their history begins with Titian and they were bequeathed to the divine family of the elect. Both these categories of artistic values are to be found in abundance and variety in the "Lola de Valence". The dress is a harmony of black, green and red; in the upper part of the garment delicate pink and light blue are brought into accord with the red of the coral necklace. But the abundance of greys is overwhelming; they are introduced in the veil and the transparent wrap, and their effect is heightened by the grey of the floor and the shoe-ribbons and by the Corot-esque grey of the fan.

But in addition to these values of colour, harmony and grey tones, there is another value present in the "Lola de Valence" which is lacking in the Delacroix and the Corot. In order to determine it, let us suppose that the colours in a picture do not tend towards one another, do not achieve reciprocal determination or blend to form a harmony, but retain their own independence and, without making any concessions, are placed beside a grey tone which, relying on its own beauty, likewise maintains its independence in the picture. There is such a picture in the Louvre, a still-life by Chardin, usually ignored and hung rather high, in which with almost the same colours as in the above-mentioned stable picture something essentially different has been achieved. In this Chardin the green of a cabbage-head and the brownish red of a piece of raw meat do not blend to form a harmony with the grey of the table-cloth. For as this grey is not, as it is in Delacroix, a colour, a derivation from white, but stands in the picture like an isolated costly object as an absolute grey tone value, it follows that the green and red likewise retain an independent existence. Instead of blending and harmony we have a contrast, which gives rise to a polyphonic melodic value. (Just as, in music, sounds which are suited to one another may occur together without combining and exist side-by-side.) This same value is found in the "Lola de Valence", where the grey, touched with pink, of the wrap, which is of considerable length and passes round the head, exists side-by-side with the sometimes greyish, sometimes brownish black of the background of theatrical scenery. It is also found at the critical point where the grey of the curtain is contrasted with the black of the dress.

If the values of colour and harmony delight our senses, and the grey tones give us inward satisfaction, the great melodic values such as we find here have the power to provide us with a vital experience, to elevate and impress our minds. It is thus possible to assign an order to such values, provided each of them is realized on an equally high level.

To sum up our impressions of the "Lola de Valence", we perceive that the greatness of Manet is due not to the luminosity and lightness of his pictures, but to the beauty of his values of colour and harmony, to the striking distinction of his abundant grey tone values, and above all to the great melodic values, the sublimest that painting can create and accessible in their highest degree only to the very greatest artists.

In the year in which he painted the "Lola", Manet rented a ramshackle studio in the Batignolles quarter. He continued to visit the Louvre, where he made the acquaintance of Berthe Morisot; he also came across Degas, who was engaged in copying Velázquez's Infanta, and exclaimed to him: "What audacity, my dear man!" In the following year he married Suzanne Leenhoff. With her, after the death of his father, he went to live in the Rue Saint-Pétersbourg, at his mother's house. At the Galerie Martinet on the Boulevard des Italiens he exhibited a few pictures. These made a great impression on certain young painters, especially on the young Claude Monet, and also on others who had met at the Atelier Gleyre and become friends, namely Sisley, Renoir and Bazille.

Most of the painters, however, together with the critics and the general public, were averse to his pictures or, worse still, abused and derided them. The tendency of the time was to emphasize the most popular categories of plastic values, those of expression and feeling, whereas Manet displayed the highest and least accessible category of artistic values—the melodic values—in a new and unaccustomed manner. The spectators sought for something in the pictures which the artist did not want to give. They focused their attention on the subject, which was miles away from Manet and did not interest him. Even his values of colour and harmony were not understood. (Delacroix was not at all popular.) The grey tones appealed to few. (Corot was at that time not universally accepted.) The melodic values, with which the greatness of Manet ultimately reached its zenith, were completely incomprehensible to all. It is possible to imagine Couture's Romans of the Decadence, but the illustrative elements in Manet's pictures seemed grotesque. Among the few admirers of "Lola de Valence" was Baudelaire, who wrote a verse in its honour which has become famous. He remained one of the fervent supporters of Manet, who painted a beautiful portrait of his friend Jeanne Duval, very much in the spirit of Baudelaire, which in a photograph looks like a work of Beardsley.

In 1863 Manet painted two masterpieces which produced an effect bordering on scandal and made his name famous in a not very enviable way. The first of these pictures was the "Déjeuner sur l'herbe". Objection was taken to the fact that a naked woman was here depicted in the company of fully-clothed men. This caused much indignation and obscured all appreciation of the beautiful brown and black of the clothes, of the distinguished grey of the trousers and the rich abundance of details in the left foreground, where Manet assembled the finest achievements of his art. When we see this picture we understand why Manet copied Titian's "Madonna with the rabbit". In the latter the isolated splendour of the grey napkin swathing the child and the bright patch of the white rabbit illuminate and give inspiration to the otherwise rather dark picture, just as, in the "Déjeuner sur l'herbe" the luminosity of the nude woman gives light and animation to the darkness of an otherwise not very remarkable forest. But that which was admired in Titian, when he brightened the landscape of his "Jupiter and Antiope" with nudes and grey draperies, that which was permitted in Courbet, when in his great picture of a studio he gave coherence to the dark confusion of the interior by means of the luminous nude, the white cat and above all the direct insertion of the brilliant beauties of grey draperies, flowing down from the naked model or lying upon the ground (the light, soul and meaning of the picture), was considered unpardonable in Manet, because nobody thought of considering the picture as anything but an indecent illustration. Refused by the Salon, it was to be seen in the neighbouring Salon des Refusés, the opening of which had been honoured with the approval of the Emperor, where, in addition to Manet, Fantin-Latour, Jongkind, Pissarro, Whistler and others also exhibited their works.

Those high artistic values which made their first appearance in a clear and pure form in his "Lola de Valence", were fulfilled and perfected in the second great picture which Manet painted in 1863, the "Olympia". With this picture Manet painted his masterpiece. Zola called it the "highest proof of his ability". Most of those who saw it went to the other extreme of incomprehension. Even Courbet disapproved of it and called the figure "a queen of spades", finding fault with the scanty modelling of the recumbent form. Later, when it was exhibited at the Salon of 1865, the critics were indignant because it contained no shadows and because bright tones were placed in juxtaposition without any transition, while the public, puzzled by the incomprehensible subject, vented its wrath on the cat, which they took in its literal sense as an object, without grasping that its significance was merely that of a black patch. The picture, as Duret relates, had the same effect on the public as a red rag on a bull. Paul de Saint-Victor wrote: "The crowd pressed forward as it does in the Morgue, to see Olympia, this slightly decomposed Olympia." And Manet, as Degas remarked, became as famous as Garibaldi.

Despite these orgies of indignation, certain young painters, who saw in Manet a new leader, expressed their warm approval. "Olympia" was painted in the year of Delacroix's death. An epoch in the history of art had ended and something new had appeared. But was it really something new? Manet did not like Delacroix, although he had copied his "Barque of Dante". In this early picture there were evidently things which interested him, and we may suppose that he was attracted not only by the luminous form of the nude woman swimming on the left, but also by the beautiful melodic value which results in the right-hand figure in the boat, when the brown of the neck and face is contrasted with the grey of the edging visible at the top of the shirt. The older Delacroix, who painted three years before his death the green, white and brown harmony of the fighting horses, did not interest him; but he was attracted by the young painter who followed the tradition of the great melodic values, and fundamentally it was this tradition which he continued. For the new element in the "Olympia", the shadowless lightness and the juxtaposition of pure tones without transitions, was in reality nothing but a necessity, without which the artist could not have created what for him were the only important things, namely the melodic values. What for him was nothing but a means towards an end, might then or later become for others the aim of a definite artistic programme.

If we were to cut Mona Lisa's smile out of Leonardo's picture, we should have merely a little piece of old canvas, darkly painted, which would produce no impression. But if we were to cut out from the "Olympia" the portion we have been discussing above, we should possess one of the most precious objects in the world, which does not merely charm us with its harmonies, but elevates the whole of our existence with its glorious melodies. Here we see the difference between those values of feeling and expression which meet with popular approval, and the great melodic values accessible only to the chosen few.

In my book "Picasso et la Tradition Française", I have endeavoured to formulate what remains to be said about the painting of this remarkable picture. "A work of this kind is not a loose combination of colour and canvas, it is not the production of an 'art-painter' whose recipes can easily be detected. These browns, greens, greys and pinks were not mixed on the palette in accordance with the dictates of professional skill and taste, nor were they purchased in a shop. On the contrary, before these superb tones could be realized in beautiful painting, a whole nation had to grow up under a determined sky, had to develop along determined lines through the centuries, and these tones had then to be grasped by a man embodying the finest characteristics of his race, possessing a heart which, like that of a noble charger, is ready for the most daring ventures, and yet remains faithful to the high school of tradition, while he must have a hand in which the culture of an old bourgeois family still lives, to give a firm and at the same time gentle form to this experience."

Among the pictures which Manet painted during this and the following year, we must mention the " Christ with Angels", undoubtedly very interesting on account of the large sheet occupying half of the picture. Manet also painted still-lifes of flowers, peonies, &c., in which, interpreting the "Olympia", he contrasted the brown of a table with the pink of the petals and the grey of a vase. He painted a bull-fight which he afterwards tore up and of which only the wonderful figure of the "Dead Toreador" in the Widerer Collection has been preserved. In this one of his most beautiful blacks comes into contact with one of the finest greys. In 1865 he painted the " Jesus mocked by the Soldiers".

In the same year, after the " Olympia" scandal, he went to Spain, where he took his fill of Velázquez, El Greco and Goya. But as a good Parisian he loathed Spanish cooking, which he considered uneatable. When he returned to France, the customs-officer at the frontier read his name on his luggage, and fetched his wife and child, in order that they might behold that strange animal about which the papers had written such terrible things. During this journey he made the acquaintance of Théodore Duret, his admirer and subsequent biographer.

During 1866 he painted pictures of Spanish subjects—bull-fights—such as so often greeted me before the war in the first room of Durand-Ruel's home, on those celebrated Tuesdays when his collection could be visited. He painted the " Matador", the " Tragedian", and above all the "Piper", which hangs opposite the " Lola" in the Camondo Collection. Zola praised the simplicity of this work, which he described as being naïve, full of grace and raw strength. The grey scarf falling from the right shoulder to the hip, and the leggings are derived from that great store-house of the Louvre, which contains the shrouds of Titian and Ribera, the towel of Rembrandt's Bathsheba, Courbet's draperies in his picture of a studio, and the table-cloths of Chardin and Cézanne. They are placed in the picture as if they were alone and had not to reckon with anything. The black of the shoes, the red of the breeches, the blue of the jacket do everything to be simple, great and strong enough to sustain the contrast with the mighty grey. If one of them is given full value, the others become lighter and tenderer, while the blue and red on the outside accord with the beautiful softer grey of the background. Very characteristic of Manet is the flute-case with its greyish, light yellow, an isolated object which has perhaps the same value as the celebrated greenish-grey glove in Titian's portrait of a young man.

It was in 1866 that Manet made the acquaintance of Monet, who had felt his influence and paid him a visit in his studio. He also got to know Cézanne and Pissarro, and Zola, who wrote an article praising him in " L'Événement", in consequence of which he lost his post as art critic to that journal. At this time Manet was a regular frequenter of the Café Guerbois in the Avenue de Clichy, where Fantin-Latour, Degas, Stevens, Zola and other painters, sculptors and literary men were wont to gather. The cultured and tranquil Fantin had been his friend for nearly ten years. In the picture he exhibited at the 1864 Salon, Fantin depicted Manet among a number of persons assembled to do honour to Delacroix. Later, in 1870, when he painted an imaginary studio at Batignolles, supposed to be that of Manet, he depicted the latter surrounded by Zola, Monet, Renoir, Bazille, Zacharie Astruc and others. In the same year the gifted Bazille, who was one of the intimates of the Manet circle and met with an untimely end in the Franco-Prussian war, introduced Manet and approximately the same group of friends into a picture showing his own studio. It is a fine piece of painting, in grey, pink and black. Another admirable work, far superior in quality to the similar garden picture by Monet, also in the Louvre, is Bazille's large picture of a family reunion in a garden, which reminds us, with its black, blue and grey, of a lighter Courbet or a darker Manet.

In 1867 an international industrial exhibition was held in Paris, but Manet was excluded from the section devoted to painting. He followed Courbet's example and exhibited his pictures close-by, in a wooden hut by the Pont de l'Alma. "Nothing but Spaniards", said Courbet, on seeing them. The catalogue comprised fifty items and an introduction written by the painter himself, in which he proclaimed his artistic sincerity. This exhibition was completely unsuccessful. In the same year Manet painted a "View of the International Exhibition" and also the celebrated picture of the execution of the Emperor Maximilien. In the following year he painted the portraits of Zola and Duret, and the "Woman with the parrot". He spent the summer in Boulogne and from there paid a visit to London. The sea and the Folkestone-Boulogne steamers appear in several of his pictures.

About this time two women played an important part in his life. Both of them frequently sat to him as models; both were painters themselves and drew inspiration from his work. Eva Gonzalès was definitely his pupil. Her life was not a long one and the number of her works is small; but several beautiful pictures by her have been preserved, notably the "Loge" at the Louvre. The other, Berthe Morisot, who could not altogether free herself from jealousy of her rival, herself ranked high in the world of art. From Manet she took only what was suited to her own strongly marked personality, and she in her turn influenced him. Her beautiful pictures are quite in accordance with the spirit and tendencies of the time, but their importance is greater than that of contemporary interest and they hold their place in the history of great painting. Paul Valéry has left us a description of this distinguished and intelligent woman: "Everything in her habits and appearance denoted distinction. As for her character, it is well known that she belonged to the rarest and most retiring class of women; she was aloof in her nature, and, unconsciously, she kept herself curiously aloof from all those who approached her, unless they happened to be the foremost artists of her time."

The year 1869 was one of the most important in his life for the art of Édouard Manet, for it brought with it both fulfilment and in a certain sense conclusion. Fulfilment, because all the elements which go to form his greatness were assembled once again in the powerful manifestation of his "Balcony". The brilliance of youth which appeals to us in the "Lola de Valence", the grandiose spontaneity of the "Olympia" are found again here, but in a more conscious form, simpler and more mature, and also richer and more concentrated. The great melodic values are piled one upon the other. Two different browns, each more precious than the other, appear in the chair and in the head of the dog, and these browns are crowned by the barely perceptible pink of the train, which in turn contrasts with the supernaturally beautiful grey of the dress worn by the seated woman, who is supposed to be Berthe Morisot. And this dress, adorned with a divine frill, contrasts at the top with another brown, that of the boy in the background; while the other shoulder stands out against the black of the male figure. In addition to this there are colour values, such as the pinkish light-yellow, of unusual beauty. In short, an abundance of the highest artistic values such as is rarely found in one picture. To find as many values as are here assembled, one would have to spend hours in the Louvre searching among the works of the very greatest masters.

The public and the critics understood nothing of all this. They were irritated by the railing and the little dog, they thought that both the women were ugly and the situation absurd. "Poor Manet is sad", wrote Berthe Morisot on this occasion. "His exhibition does not please the public taste; and that always astonishes him every time." After such a fulfilment, no further development in this direction was possible. We must mention a portrait of Eva Gonzalès and one or two pictures of a delicate beauty which represent Manet's farewell to this period of his work: the "Lunch in the studio", with the young man wearing a yellow straw-hat (his brother-in-law, Leenhoff) and leaning against a table, a picture dominated by black and grey; and the "Young man with the soap-bubble", in which Manet realizes once again his lovely "blond" grey, and in which the distinction of the drawing testifies once more to the tenderness of a great heart and the impulse of a great soul. The history of the great Manet whom we love and honour, who has enriched our lives by adding to the greatest possessions of mankind, is now over. From now on begins the story of the great virtuoso Manet whose skill we admire.

After Blériot had flown the Channel, and Lindbergh had later emulated him by crossing the Atlantic in a much-improved machine, they both devoted themselves to the technical development of their experiments. The prodigious effort of the achievement itself could not be repeated again. In the same way Manet, after reaching with his "Lola", his "Olympia" and his "Balcony" the heights of ecstasy, of incomparable beauty and of inexhaustible abundance, was obliged to come down to earth again. He too had done something which can be accomplished only once. It is true that there have been masters—for instance Titian and Rembrandt—who succeeded in maintaining the same high level until the end of their lives. But if in their works the highest artistic values remained constantly alive, this was because they were combined with the less sublime plastic and minor artistic values. Their art thus remained in touch with the earth. If in the "Bathsheba", through the juxtaposition of the most beautiful brown and the most beautiful green to be found in the whole Louvre, a perfect melodic value ensues, surpassing everything created by God on earth or by man in the heaven of art, nevertheless the picture retains its earthly side, because this highest value, perceptible only to the competent few, is accompanied, owing to the legend depicted and the expression of the countenance, by the popular values of feeling and expression.

In Manet's great period, however, such values are completely absent. He was interested only in the highest and most difficult values, the great melodic values and after them the values of grey tones. To a smaller extent the values of colour and harmony also interested him. But the values of feeling and expression are lacking. His figures, considered as human beings, are uninteresting. Olympia's face is blank; she has nothing to tell us. All human relationship between the figures of the "Déjeuner sur l'herbe" is absent. We feel that the people standing on the balcony do not know each other at all. The soldiers in the painting of Jesus and those in the "Execution of the Emperor Maximilien" are Parisian types who have no spiritual connection with the event depicted. Even the other plastic values are hardly represented. The spatial values are not interesting; everything is crowded together. Movement is completely absent; the pictures are static, the attitudes rigid.

The Manet of this period stood alone in his time. One or two of the great masters of the past might have understood him and have recognized him as one of their peers. The painters of his own time who loved him did so because he painted in light colours and had no shadows in his pictures, and because he inserted colour after colour without transitions. Fundamentally they did not understand him at all. And he for his part did not think much of his friends, the "Impressionists". Their painting scarcely interested him. He even wanted to avoid making Renoir's acquaintance because he considered his pictures bad. And when he did get to know him, he wanted Monet to try and persuade Renoir to give up painting because he had so little talent for it. He endeavoured at all costs to avoid exhibiting his pictures together with those of Cézanne. Similarly he did his best to avoid exhibiting in common with the other Impressionists. In such circumstances disagreements were inevitable. He felt the difference in rank. What interested him was not their painting, but their experiments—the "plein-air" and the disintegration of colours. For this reason Monet, the most conscientious worker among them, was nearest to him; from him he could learn more than from the others. In the future he would have other means of introducing light into a picture than those he employed in the "Déjeuner sur l'herbe", where the light-coloured nude is like a lamp burning in a dark landscape. His technical ability mastered the new methods with remarkable rapidity and thoroughness. It might happen that in some of his pictures the tricks of art were greater than the work of art. His position was determined by the works of his first period. The lofty flight which had brought him fame was over, and he could not have attempted it again. The new element which entered his work had nothing to do with what had gone before; it served merely to enlarge the range of his means. With fine intuition Jacques Émile Blanche remarked that for Manet Impressionism and "Plein-air" were not the lightning flashes of divine grace; they helped him to become the great virtuoso in whom the passion for values was replaced by the interest in methods, the great creator giving way to the great organizer of the means at his disposal.

During his earlier period Manet had almost invariably painted in his studio and, like Corot, made sketches in the open air. After his "View of the International Exhibition", he sometimes painted from nature, for example the sea at Boulogne. But we must remember that Manet was and remained a Parisian and did not, like the Impressionists, make excursions into the environs. The first picture of considerable size which he painted in the open was probably the portrait of the Impressionist painter De Nittis with his family, with whom he stayed in the country in 1870. The sun shining on the faces and the stretches of turf, with the play of its coloured patches, induced him to paint this picture.

The Franco-Prussian war interrupted his artistic activities. He became a staff-officer of the National Guard and served under the command of Meissonier, who adopted a cool attitude towards him and did not treat him as a colleague. Later, on the occasion of one of Meissonier's exhibitions, Manet had his revenge. "That is good, really good," he said, "everything is of steel except the cuirass." During the siege of Paris and the Commune, he joined his mother and his wife, who had gone to Oloron in the Pyrenees. He painted, in the open air, the gulf of Arcachon and the harbour of Bordeaux. On his return to Paris Stevens arranged the sale of two of his pictures to Durand-Ruel. A little later Manet himself sold this dealer twenty-two of his pictures for a total of 35,000 francs. He needed money, for his share in his father's inheritance was dwindling.

The summer of 1872 he spent in Holland, where he studied Frans Hals. In Paris, he had left the Rue Guyot and rented a large room as a studio in the Rue Saint-Pétersbourg. In 1873 he painted "Le bon Bock" (the good glass of beer), externally influenced by Frans Hals, and in other respects not very "Manet", because a different series of values, not found in his other works, here takes the upper hand, namely the values of feeling and expression. The comfortable aspect of the fat bourgeois smoking his pipe and drinking his beer ("Haarlem beer", Stevens maliciously called it, referring to the influence of Frans Hals) awakes "Stimmung" in the spectator. For this reason the picture cut a good figure in the Salon. But in other ways too a new order of artistic values was entering Manet's work, the fruit of the "plein-air" and disintegration of colour experiments. It interested him to construct space out of air and light, and the pictures painted in this year, among them the "Game of Croquet"—like many others painted during the following years at Calais and Berck, such as the "Swallows"—show a very exact calculation of distances. These spatial values are realized very often with a minimum of external expedients, more with the help of the atmosphere than by means of the persons and objects depicted. As sun and light give them animation, his pictures lose their static element and become naturally filled with movement.

It is not surprising that in proportion as these categories of plastic values penetrated into Manet's works, certain artistic values, which in his early works had predominated alone, tended to disappear, namely the grey tone values and the melodic values. At times the early colour elements reappeared, but with a very different effect. In 1872 he had painted a little picture of Berthe Morisot holding a black fan in her hand and seated on a chair, dressed in black, with pink shoes. It is true that we find here the black which afterwards was never absent from his pictures, as well as the pink, but no melodic value results, while the dress is cleverly set off against a reddish background, which is not even interesting as a simple colour value. Here it is the clever trick of a great artist which excites our admiration. But we think with regret of the backgrounds of the "Lola" and the "Piper", and of another picture, similar in subject to this portrait of Berthe Morisot but painted seven years before: the "Angélina"—also known as the "Young woman at her window"—where another feminine hand is holding a fan, forming, with the black of the fan, the grey of the cuff and the brown of the dress, a melodic value, which, simpler and severer than that of the "Olympia", produces with its simplicity an impression equal to that which the hand of Olympia produces with its magnificence. But whereas the latter hand remains alone and uncomprehended in the rich history of beautiful hands, that of Berthe Morisot fulfils no higher function and must be assigned to the category of the objects of clever and brilliant painting, such as are to be found in so many pictures. This is the beginning of that Manet who could influence others both in France and abroad, the Manet who could also inspire English and German painters.

This change of direction in his art is probably connected with the fact that his fame now attracted crowds of people to his studio. About this time, when he painted the "Ball at the Opéra", he was visited not only by numerous models, but also by fashionable painters, by the demi-monde and by well-known bankers and financiers. One important relationship must be noted: his friendship with Stéphane Mallarmé, whom he met in the evenings at the Café de la Nouvelle-Athènes in the Place Pigalle.

Manet had followed so zealously the experiments of his Impressionist friends that, in 1874, when the group exhibited together and the word "Impressionist" was used for the first time, he too had painted a picture in which the new aspirations were realized. He had visited Monet and his family at Argenteuil, examining Monet's pictures with the keenest interest and learning much from them. Of Renoir, on the other hand, who was likewise at Argenteuil, he said: "Ah, the unfortunate man! What he does is fearful. He will never make anything of it." The "Impressionistic" picture which Manet painted he called "Monet in his studio", though "studio" must here be understood as meaning the boat in which at that time Monet was painting his wife. The picture called "Argenteuil" which he painted there was also in accordance with the precepts of the new school. The raw sunlight and the glaring blue of the water caused the greatest indignation at the Salon.

In the same year, 1874, Manet went to Venice, where he painted several pictures of the Grand Canal; during the following years he produced his "Washing Day" and "The Artist" (the etcher Desboutin), which were rejected by the Salon. For this reason he exhibited them in the Rue Saint-Pétersbourg, and sent out personal invitations to view them. About the same time he painted Faure in the role of Hamlet, the portrait of Mallarmé and the celebrated "Nana". The last-named picture was also rejected by the Salon, or rather removed from it. That a gentleman in a top-hat should be seated by the side of a half-dressed lady, aroused the same indignation as the female nude with the fully-dressed men in the "Déjeuner sur l'herbe" had previously done. The picture itself has the qualities of the subject it depicts, that is to say charm, beauty and elegance, and, like the subject, it appealed to a wider public.

16

Manet now left the studio in the Rue Saint-Pétersbourg and took another in the Rue d'Amsterdam. By this time he was a famous man, but still not recognized for what he really was and not understood. On the occasion of another international exhibition, his works were once more refused admission. Again he thought of holding a private exhibition, but his means did not allow him to put this idea into execution. He had small worries as well as greater ones. Degas had painted a picture of him listening to his wife who is playing at the piano. Manet thought that he himself had been painted well, but that the figure of his wife was a failure, so he cut it out of the picture. Degas took this badly and sent back a still-life which Manet had presented to him.

Of the important pictures of his last years we must mention the "Greenhouse", painted in 1879. The drawing in this work is fine and the brushwork distinguished. Tschudi mentions the fresh complexion and the soft delicacy of the feminine form; he praises the poise and mimicry of the man, and lastly the "colouristic taste" of the picture. It was evidently a period of artistic creation when it was difficult to say anything but trivialities which might be applied to a thousand other pictures. Nevertheless it is rather distressing to find the word "taste" applied to the painter of "Olympia". The notable impression which the picture produces must be attributed not so much to clearly definable artistic values as to the mastery, the imposing domination of technical devices which is here achieved.

In the same year he painted Clemenceau; in the following year the portrait of his friend Antonin Proust, who in 1881 became Minister of Fine Arts. This is a studio picture with a distinguished bearing, effective in the sparingness of the means employed. It thus forms a contrast to the "plein-air" picture of the same year, "Chez le père Lathuille", in which Manet's clever and purposeful hand is as prodigal with its gifts as his great heart used to be. Air and light emphasize the colour values, create space and introduce movement. And the values of feeling and expression, to which Manet also paid attention in this picture, are realized better than in the "Greenhouse", where two models unsuccessfully endeavour to establish a human relationship.

To this period belong also the Impressionistic "Rue de Berne" and the portrait of Rochefort, and also that of Pertuiset, the lion-hunter, which to a certain extent forms with "Le bon Bock" a category apart and, like the latter, helped to augment his popularity and his fame. It also brought him a medal from the Salon and the award of the Legion of Honour. Under the title of "Jeanne" or "Spring" we also find a portrait of a delightful Parisienne which pleased the public.

Since 1880 Manet had been aware of the first traces of an illness which brought a disturbing element into his life and his work—symptoms of paralysis in one of his legs. This explains the fact that from then on he painted more often than before flowers and still-lifes, and especially pastels of friends, acquaintances and beautiful women. At that time nobody wanted to possess or pay for these pastels, which to-day are much sought after and of considerable value. At this point we may mention that there exists by Manet's hand a not very large number of lithographs, and also etchings, for instance of the "Lola" and the "Olympia". Drawings, too, have been preserved, in which he recorded the characteristics of a moment.

In 1882, when his illness grew more serious, he rented a villa at Rueil, taking his mother and his wife to live there. Wrong treatment of his disease and a lack of resistance which may be traced back to his descent from an old and exhausted family, hastened his end. After the amputation of a leg, which he was too ill to realize, he died on April 30th, 1883.

He painted one more great work at the end of his life, one year before he died. This was the "Bar at the Folies-Bergère", a brilliant piece of fireworks, with colours and harmonies scattered all over the canvas, in which the clever use of a mirror revealed hitherto unsuspected spatial values. It is the work of the greatest virtuoso of his time, who was also one of the greatest creators of all times.

:

The picture had no success on account of the absence of narrative content, which the public is so unwilling to dispense with. Albert Wolff, the foremost critic of the time, wrote of the picture with reserved appreciation. Manet thanked him, and added that before his death he would like to read his obituary notice written by the same hand.

We find this obituary notice in the "Figaro" of May 1st, 1883, the day after Manet's death. It ends with the words: "To have left two pre-eminent pictures, worthy to be saluted with the applause of French art, that is sufficient fame for any artist." The two pictures, in the opinion of the writer of the article, were the "Child with a sword" and "Le bon Bock".

We, however, prefer to say that Manet, with his "Lola de Valence", his "Olympia", his "Balcony" and many other admirable paintings of the highest quality, has inscribed his name in the history of the painting of all times and all nations. There it will remain for ever and above it one might place the words:

"Manet et manebit."

Drawing by Édouard Manet: Portrait of Monet

II.

IMPRESSIONISTS

The artistic values in painting lie between two opposite poles. In the Louvre there are two pictures, each of which exemplifies in an incomparable manner one of these poles: Leonardo's Mona Lisa and Rembrandt's Bathsheba, which we mentioned in the preceding chapter. In the Mona Lisa we find the most popular values of all, those of feeling and expression, realized in the most perfect manner possible. In the Bathsheba, at the point where the grey of a sheet of paper is set off against the brown of a shadow, we have the most exclusive of artistic values, a melodic value which recalls the polyphonies of Johann Sebastian Bach. Whereas in the former picture we have a case where painting approaches literature, in the latter it enters the field of music. The smile of the Mona Lisa has a certain material importance, but when we experience the melodic value of the Rembrandt picture, we forget that we have before us a piece of paper and a shadow. In the former picture the essential element is found in external life, in the latter it lies in the loneliness of a great soul.

Corot and Manet sometimes abandoned their studios, that is to say their solitude and remoteness from the world, in order to obtain material from nature, with which, on their return, they realized their values of grey tones or great melodies. It was a material which they took seriously, a reality which they loved, the formal substance of life. But the fact that they usually remained in their studios proves that they sought the centre of gravity in themselves and, once they had found it, could not be persuaded to abandon it. The Impressionists left their studios to go out into the open air, and they remained there. In the studio, that is to say in themselves, there was nothing so important that they could not abandon it. Their more modest temperaments relied on chance and whatever it might bring. They joined forces with the most changeable, the most restless and unreliable of all elements, the sun. The sun deprives objects of their substance and weight, in other words of their essence, and in return gives them an external appearance or "look". This excursion into the open air, which never came to an end, was bound up with their duty towards the surface of things.

When Manet in the latter part of his life also left his studio and established himself in the open air and the sunlight, he had to leave his heavy baggage behind him, namely the greatness of his soul. The baggage of the Impressionists was lighter. On those excursions which played such a large part in their lives, Pissarro could easily take with him the humanity of his heart, Sisley his delicacy, Monet his poetry and Renoir his eroticism. As well as the greatness of his soul, Manet also left behind him in the studio the greatness of his values. In the latter half of his life, he busied himself with the values of colour and harmony, and these were values which were accessible to the Impressionists as well.

We must not attribute an exaggerated importance to the Impressionistic experiment. Lightness in itself and the disintegration of colours have only a relative importance. Inside their own epoch they represented a step forward, for they denoted the end of a kind of painting which Zola characterized with the words "Romans and Greeks made of mahogany" and "porcelain nymphs". Impressionism began at the moment when Corot was breathing his last. No one can maintain that in this way something better took the place of that which had become old-fashioned, nor would anyone dare to assert that Rembrandt is inferior to the Impressionists because he painted "dark" whereas they painted "light". Impressionism is merely the mode of expression, impossible to assess, of a certain epoch, preceded and followed by other modes of expression. The value of Impressionism is in relation to the value of the artists who practised it, greater in some of them, less in others. Nevertheless it must be noted that the methods of Corot and Courbet offered still greater possibilities in themselves to artists of ability, while the Impressionistic method was in general sufficient for the artists who made use of it.

Nowadays the nature of the experiment is a matter of common knowledge. It aimed at reproducing objects not in their material aspect but in the coloured analysis created by sun, light and air. Local colours therefore disappear and are replaced by a multitude of tiny points of colour into which the painter has disintegrated them; these, to the eyes of the spectator, join together again and form a unity. Connected with this is the fact that the shadows are no longer black, but blue, violet or lilac. The colours alter according to the influence of the atmosphere, according to whether nature is tranquil or a wind is blowing, whether the sky is clear or overcast, the air dry or damp. In these landscapes we can judge the time of day as if with the aid of a watch; with a thermometer we could almost tell the temperature and with a barometer forecast the probable weather.

Impressionism in the wider sense had already existed in earlier times, and Piero della Francesca has rightly been recalled in this connection. In the narrower sense, mention must be made of Constable and Turner, whom our Impressionists had opportunity of seeing in London and to whose influence they were subject. Especially Constable. Turner they abandoned after a time; Monet felt that his influence was un-productive, and Renoir called him a confectioner. Even Delacroix had transformed the play of light and shade into colour harmonies and served as a pattern for the Impressionists. In 1860 an exhibition of the works of Velázquez was held in Paris. The grey which predominates in them, and which also interested the Impressionists in the works of Chardin, was for them less important as an element of aesthetic value than as an element of light colouring. In this sense they were also influenced by Manet. Nothing, however, shows that they understood his real greatness; they took him as a model because of the light colouring of his pictures. Another important factor which encouraged them in their efforts was the Japanese wood-cut, which began to be known in Paris in the early 'sixties, and had attracted the interest of wider circles by the time of the international exhibition in 1867. People began to collect these woodcuts. Edmond de Goncourt wrote his book on Outamaro. The light, the brightness, the colour harmonies taken from nature, won the approval of the Impressionists.

Their own leanings and the influences to which they were subjected, which encouraged them in these leanings, determined the scale of artistic values characteristic of the Impressionists. These were, in the first place, the values of feeling and expression, which were what they sought for in nature. However much their art (probably as a result of the " experiment ") may seem at a first glance to resemble " art for art's sake ", in reality it is nearer the point at which art approaches literature. They wanted to obtain " Stim-mung ". They wanted to reproduce the " smile of the Mona Lisa " through the medium of a landscape in the light of the rising or setting sun, or by means of the softly illuminated figure of a nude girl.

The restlessness of the sun, which illuminates first one thing and then another and dissolves the per-manence of objects, the wind which rises in their pictures, the air which they cause to vibrate, the entirely " uninterrupted " life which they depict, create by themselves marked values of movement, which have great importance in the works of the Impressionists. The same may be said of the spatial values, which are realized not by linear perspective, but by the atmospherically perceptible distances resulting from light and air.

That the tactile values are lacking in artists who avoid everything tangible and represent not the objects themselves, but their appearance, is not surprising. Nor is the fact that all compositional values are neglected. No feeling for rhythm and no ordered distribution of the volumes determine the formation of the plane. Everything is left to chance. Artistic intention is sacrificed and replaced by the caprices of nature.

A natural consequence of this experiment was that Impressionism brought with it an enrichment of the colour values. The disintegration of the local colours gave rise to the creation of an abundance of nuances. But the quality of the colour values did not improve in proportion to the quantity. The accidents

20

of nature, which they had constantly before their eyes, and the necessities inherent to the experiment itself were for them of greater importance than the deliberate creations of artistic fantasy. The material beauty of the colours often suffered from this, and instead of harmonic values we find in many of their landscapes nothing but a painful effort on the part of the colours to agree with one another.

Nevertheless, there were moments in the lives of these artists when they aspired to "higher things", when their creative power and genius strove to achieve something outside the fixed limits of the Impressionistic experiment. At such times they deviated a little from the experiment and endeavoured to shake off the fetters of a fixed idea. "There is not a single little process which can be turned into a formula", said Renoir to Vollard. And Florent Fels relates that Monet, to whom Impressionism owes most, spoke the following words, which I quote from an article by Jacques Émile Blanche: "One cannot make pictures with doctrines," and "technique changes but art remains the same." That Cézanne, to whom a special volume in this series will be devoted, did not want to be considered an Impressionist, is well known.

Perhaps, then, there was no such thing as Impressionism in the sense of a great positive fact? Perhaps what was then and is still to-day called Impressionism was in reality nothing but a new (and not even quite new) method of presenting certain artistic values of only moderate quality? Perhaps its importance was serious only for minor painters who achieved fame by means of a catchword, because it helped them to be associated with famous names such as Renoir or Manet; or for dealers who could do good business with this catchword, because pictures which obviously conformed to a "tendency" were easier to sell than others? However this may be, the fact remains that the word "Impressionism" was not invented by the painters themselves; it was a derisive epithet applied to them by a layman; at first they did not like it at all, and it was only later that they decided to adopt it.

Under the title of "Société Anonyme des artistes peintres, sculpteurs et graveurs", Pissarro, Monet, Sisley, Renoir, Berthe Morisot, Cézanne, Guillaumin, together with Degas, Boudin, Lépine and others, held a combined exhibition in 1874 on the Boulevard des Capucines, at the premises of the photographer Nadar. To this Monet sent a picture which he called "Impression. Soleil levant". This title inspired a critic of the "Charivari" to invent the word "Impressionist"—a term of abuse which caught on at once and was used by everybody except the painters themselves. The moral result of this exhibition was a scandal, the material result a catastrophe. At an auction held in 1875 seventy pictures were sold for little more than 10,000 francs. When Durand-Ruel, that wise and courageous dealer, organized an exhibition in the following year, Albert Wolff, whose obituary notice of Manet we mentioned above, wrote the following remarkable words, which are quoted by Duret, in the "Figaro": "The Rue Le Peletier is unlucky. After the fire at the Opéra, a new misfortune has befallen this quarter. An exhibition has just been opened at Durand-Ruel's which calls itself an exhibition of painting. The unsuspecting passer-by enters and his eyes are confronted by an appalling spectacle. Five or six lunatics, one of them a woman, have found a rendezvous in which to exhibit their works."

The first exhibition held under the name of "Impressionists" took place in the following year in the Rue Le Peletier. Seventeen artists were represented with 241 works. The public greeted it with loud laughter. Crowds assembled jeeringly round the pictures, and only in the case of Cézanne's works did their laughter turn to indignation and abuse. Duret relates that an auction held in the same year brought in 7,600 francs for forty-five pictures. Exhibitions were held in various places during the following years. In 1883, Durand-Ruel, whose means were gradually being exhausted in the struggle, held special exhibitions from March to June, in premises rented for the purpose on the Boulevard de la Madeleine, of the works of Monet, Renoir, Pissarro and Sisley. The last combined exhibition of Impressionists took place three years later. After this things began to get better and the supporters of the new movement increased in numbers. About the middle of the 'nineties the period of complete success set in.

The painters with whom we are concerned here sprang from those categories of the petite bourgeoisie which have given so many glorious names to France in every sphere of activity. Restraint, aversion to excess either in intellectual or physical matters, a simple masculine pride devoid of vanity, an honest insistence on their artistic convictions despite poverty and misfortune, characterized them all. During a long lifetime they fought shoulder to shoulder for their common interests and at the same time cultivated what was individually characteristic of each. Intimately related to the beautiful sky and the gentle earth of the Île-de-France, they have preserved its localities and its rivers for all times in paintings which are eminently French.

The oldest among them was C a m i l l e   P i s s a r r o, who was born in 1830 on the island of St. Thomas in the Antilles, the son of a French Israelite. He came to Paris as a young man and under the tuition of a certain Monsieur Savary at a pension in Passy he cultivated a taste for drawing. On his return to St. Thomas, this hobby did not fit in with the profession of merchant for which he was intended. He tried to combine the two as well as he could, until one day the Danish painter Fritz Melby took him to Caralos, where he was able to paint and draw. On attaining his majority in 1855, he returned to Paris and came into personal contact with Corot, who gave him advice and encouragement. He also became acquainted with Monet and Cézanne, and saw the works of Delacroix and Courbet at the international exhibition.

In 1859 we find him at Montmorency, and later at La Varenne-Saint-Hilaire and Pontoise. His pictures at this time are dark grey and green, full of earnest feeling and painted in the open air. He exhibited them at the Salon, and once at the Salon des Refusés. They have the simple, tranquil and timeless character of Corot's pictures, and an air of distinction undisturbed by any experiment. Under the influence of Manet, whom Pissarro got to know personally in 1866, his palette became lighter. His association with Renoir, Monet and Sisley loosened the forms in his landscapes, and gave him understanding for the eternal flow of things, the changing influence of time. He thus drew away from Corot externally, but he retained the latter's great feeling, his love of the sky and his attachment to the earth. His pictures remained what they had been before, documents of the human heart.

After his marriage, Pissarro settled at Louveciennes, in a house on the road leading from Saint-Germain to Versailles. During the Franco-Prussian war and the Commune he was in London, and when he came back he found his house occupied by the Germans; several hundred pictures had disappeared, supposedly destroyed by fire. Even before the war his financial position had been very bad and now it was no better. At that time "Père Martin" had bought small pictures from him for forty francs; now it was the turn of Durand-Ruel and "Père Tanguy", but they had difficulty in re-selling his pictures, while the exhibition together with the other Impressionists at Nadar's in 1874 brought him nothing but derision and abuse. In the meantime Pissarro had moved to Pontoise.

In the pictures he painted at this time the local colours are disintegrated, but the human figures, houses and trees retain their firm outlines, for example in the large garden picture of 1874, in which a woman, a child, flower-beds, a tree, an overcast sky and even the vibrating air provide us with beautiful values of feeling and make us forget the experimental elements. He painted in this manner the banks of the Oise, the humble dwellings and the little vegetable-gardens. The humility of the subjects and his love for them give these pictures a soulful spirituality. But it was precisely this Franciscan note which alienated the public, who wanted pathos and literary sensations in painting. Pissarro often met Cézanne, who was painting in Auvers, and they influenced each other reciprocally.

In 1883 Pissarro moved to Éragny-Bazincourt. He painted the fields, peasants and fruit-picking, not with the literary sentimentality of Millet, but with the same simplicity with which God had created them. At the same time he pursued the experiment to its ultimate consequences. In general he was its master, but sometimes it gained the upper hand over the artistic side of his nature. Even then, however, one thing

1. ÉDOUARD MANET: YOUTHFUL PORTRAIT OF ANTONIN PROUST

2. ÉDOUARD MANET: THE ABSINTHE DRINKER

3. ÉDOUARD MANET: LOLA OF VALENCIA

4. ÉDOUARD MANET: CONCERT IN THE TUILERIES GARDENS ("LA MUSIQUE AUX TUILERIES")

always remained: the beauty of the sky of the Île-de-France; and side-by-side with the values of feeling, there appeared, distributed in little groups over the surface, values of colour-harmony.

When he was sixty-six years old, his eyesight began to fail. From this time on he painted views of towns from behind closed windows: the quays at Rouen; the Avenue de l'Opéra in Paris from the Hôtel du Louvre; the Tuileries Gardens from a window in the Rue de Rivoli; the Place Dauphine and the Pont-Neuf. He also painted views of Dieppe and Le Havre.

He died in 1903, just when he was about to begin a new series of Parisian views. There is a self-portrait, painted in that year, in which he is standing with his back to the window, through which the busy street is visible. The patriarchal head and the long white beard symbolize the wisdom and goodness which were the essential features of his character and which distinguished his life both in happiness and in misfortune.

At one time there was a tendency—a very bad one—to assign Pissarro to the second class among the Impressionists. But he had a warmer heart than any of them, and he felt and realized better than the others those values of feeling and expression to which they all attached so much importance.

As regards his age, the second of the Impressionists was Alfred Sisley, who was born in Paris in 1839. His family was of English origin, and when he was eighteen he went to England, to learn the language and prepare himself for a commercial career. But he showed little aptitude for his father's profession. He had artistic leanings, which were further encouraged when he met Monet, Bazille and Renoir at the Atelier Gleyre. The financial position of his parents enabled him to devote himself to painting without the necessity of earning his living thereby. Like the other Impressionists he preferred Paris and its environs, and lived for some time at Louveciennes and Bougival.

During the Franco-Prussian war his father died, and the financial position of the family was completely changed. Before he had been the most fortunate of all, but now his fate was a hard one. He was married and had a wife and children to keep. Till 1875 we find him in these difficult circumstances, painting at Voisins and Marly. His pictures fetched about a hundred francs at auctions and the smaller ones he sold, if he could, for thirty or forty francs. Duret tells us of a letter in which Sisley asked him to find a collector who would give him three thousand francs for thirty pictures, with the right to choose what he liked. In this way Sisley hoped to be able to live and work for six months. His was a noble nature, and he bore every sacrifice without making the slightest concession in his painting.

During the following years, after a visit to England, he lived in Sèvres, and in 1879 he settled at Moret. During the latter part of his life he visited Normandy and painted in the neighbourhood of Rouen, and a few years later on the Welsh coast. When he wanted to become naturalized in 1895, it was found that he did not possess the necessary papers. He died in 1899 in bad circumstances, but when the pictures he left were auctioned, twenty-seven of them brought in more than 112,000 francs, and a little later, in 1900, an important picture by him was sold for the imposing sum of 43,000 francs.

The subjects of his pictures were determined by the various places he lived in. In addition to the landscapes of fields, meadows, and rivers such as are to be found all over the Île-de-France, he painted floods at Port-Marly, snow-scenes at Louveciennes, views of the village of Voisins, of the Thames, the little river at Moret and the village itself with its churches and bridges.

His artistic personality was subject to two essential influences: Corot and Manet. His own delicacy and sensibility attracted him to the former, and his interest in the contemporary Impressionistic formulas to the latter. The plastic values of expression and the other values which play so large a part in Impressionism tended to weaken the influence of Corot, but the latter is more perceptible in Sisley than in any other of the Impressionists. While Pissarro usually created his values of feeling and expression through the beautiful realization of light, air and sky, and soon replaced a noble array of grey, green and greyish-blue

CLAUDE MONET

tones with other more neutral and material colour values, the beautiful material of colour remained an essential element in Sisley's painting. Moreover, grey tone values sometimes appear. In his lovely picture of a bridge, in the Louvre, they are present in many variations. Browns and pinks are found in his works which remind us of Corot's Italian palette, and of his hand too, for they are inserted with similar delicacy, in order to form a house or a tree. (Nevertheless, compared with the Corot of the best period, everything seems attenuated, of less unequivocal beauty.) But other colour values also appear, light-blue, black, a particular kind of light-red, and light-green. There are beautiful harmonic values, and whole portions which one would like to cut out and preserve as precious jewels. There is much in his pictures which might be dispensed with. However beautiful his houses, bridges, trees and expanses of snow may be in themselves, we often find in the same picture patches smeared or dabbed on, which have no other meaning than that of purely literary "Stimmung". And there are whole pictures too, as is the case with all the other artists of this school, of which the same may be said.

The most consistent representative of Impressionism was Claude Monet, who was born in Paris in 1840. He spent his youth at Le Havre, where his father was a merchant and where he made the acquaintance of Boudin and Jongkind, who later influenced his painting. His desire to become a painter brought him into conflict with his father. But after his health had broken down when he went to Africa as a "Chasseur d'Afrique", he succeeded in getting his own way and entered the Atelier Gleyre as a pupil. He remained there barely a year. About this time he saw Manet's pictures at Martinet's on the Boulevard des Italiens, and was deeply impressed by them. Hitherto his own pictures, some of which he had exhibited at the time when Manet was showing his "Olympia", had been dark. He painted landscapes of Normandy and views of Paris, among the latter (1866) the church of Saint-Germain-l'Auxerrois, one of the most beautiful pictures produced at this time and one which no one who has ever seen it can forget. He also painted a number of large figure compositions, an open-air luncheon-party, the celebrated "Camille" in a black and green silk dress, and the Japanese girl in a red dress. Two years later he painted an indoor luncheon-party, after which he gave up figure-painting.

From Paris he moved to Argenteuil, where he painted the Seine for several years. The war compelled him to leave and he went to Holland, where he found a new inspiration in Japanese engravings and in drawings by Hiroshige, which later influenced him considerably, for example in his series of poplars. In Holland he painted windmills, and in 1873 one of his finest pictures, the canal at Saardam. In between, in 1871, he visited London, painting the city and the Thames. He then returned to Argenteuil, where in 1875 he painted the beautiful picture now in the Camondo Collection and many other landscapes.

His palette had become lighter, sun and light flowed into his pictures, and in 1874 he exhibited the landscape from which the word "Impressionism" was derived. His financial position was desperate— despite the fact that Durand-Ruel, whom he had met in London, took an interest in him. Manet came to the rescue. In Paris he painted the celebrated "Gare Saint-Lazare", with its blue haze, a masterpiece of Impressionistic painting. In 1878 he moved to Vétheuil, and here were created those numerous pictures, each with different lighting, of the little riverside town—always the same section every time—which are the first things one thinks of when the name of Monet is mentioned. After the exhibition on the Boulevard de la Madeleine in 1883, where he showed fifty-six pictures, had awakened a slight but promising interest in his work, we find him in the winter of the following year at Bordighera, where he introduced into his pictures the blue sea and the earth sparkling with colour. Water always attracted him. Two years later, at Belle-Île, he painted the sea with the cliffs and rocks.

Later on in his life, too, he always showed a preference for water, in every kind of surroundings: in 1888 he was at Antibes, in 1895 in Norway, at the turn of the century in London again, painting the Thames, and in 1908, when he was sixty-eight years old, in Venice. But since 1886 his home had been at

24

Giverny, where there was plenty of water—the Seine and its tributary the Epte, and the ponds with water-lilies in the splendid wild-flower gardens he had laid out. Here he painted his series of water-lilies with the Japanese bridge, in all lightings and at all hours of the day, just as previously he had painted other series—the haycocks, Rouen cathedral, and the poplars.

A few years after he had settled in Giverny, his circumstances changed for the better, there was an end to want, he earned plenty of money and strangers came in crowds to see him. Claude Monet died in 1926 with the reputation of a great master, one of the glories of France.

This man, who left behind him numerous much-admired works, had lived the life of an honest bourgeois and a conscientious craftsman of painting. He had passed through misery and glory with the same equanimity, he had made no concessions in his art, he was a faithful friend, and one could pay him the finest tribute that can be paid to any man, namely that he was severe with himself and gentle with others. His long and productive life seemed to have passed with the constant rhythm of a great river. Yet when we read the notes which his friend Clemenceau wrote about him, we perceive that there were dark hours in the life of this great artist, during which he suffered torture and destroyed many of his works.

Then too, when we examine his work, we see a tragic line running from the magnificence of his Saint-Germain-l'Auxerrois to the petty artistic feats of his pictures of Rouen Cathedral, from a small and admirable still-life of ham in the Louvre to the pretentious fireworks of the water-lilies in the Tuileries. Seldom has the art of so gifted and so strong-minded a painter sunk from such heights to such depths.

Only a tragic schism in his artistic formation can explain this descent, which the foolish instincts of a stupid public applauded. Only the fact that in him various sources existed side-by-side, competing with one another instead of uniting, can provide us with the key to this remarkable phenomenon.

Examining his early works, we find—in addition to the Saint-Germain-l'Auxerrois—a number of pictures in which grey tone values like those of Corot and colour values in brown and pink are applied with the sensitiveness of a hand obeying the dictates of a great heart. We find these simple colour values down to his Dutch period, each of them a confession and betraying, with the combination of harmonies, a definite state of mind. The sensations we experience on beholding these pictures are derived, not from any literary interest, but from purely artistic sources. And we can understand how Monet, on seeing Corot's "Woman with the mandolin", that marvel of grey tone values, could whisper to Clemenceau: "I like that better than the Gioconda."

Nevertheless in the soul of Monet the Mona Lisa triumphed over the "Woman with the mandolin". For Monet was what is called a "poet". The values of feeling and expression superseded those of colour and harmony in his work. He sought for "Stimmung". Sometimes this was combined with the values of colour and harmony, but too often he was content with coloured lumps of cotton-wool, dabs and streaks of colour which give the effect of morning and evening atmosphere, or senseless neutral colours which result in illustrations full of sentiment. Thus he created his series of haycocks, poplars, cathedral pictures and water-lilies. The particular "poetry" of every hour of the day was captured. It was as if Leonardo had painted the Mona Lisa with twenty different expressions, one version after the other: smiling, laughing, sad, worried, sulky, affectionate, cheerful, happy, distraite, frightened, &c. In this way it was only natural that whole series of superfluous pictures should result, but it also comes about that in one cathedral picture a particularly beautiful light-blue and light-yellow colour value, inserted at the right place by a happy turn of composition, combines to form a perfect harmonic value. The first-rate creator and the poet might come into accord from time to time, but all too often it was the latter who drove the former from the field.

There was a third source of inspiration, and not the least of the three, from which the master drew strength: his eye. Monet's eye was perhaps the best of his century, for it was keen, curious, intelligent and educated to the discipline of the disintegration of colours into an incredible number of nuances. It rendered great services to the Impressionistic experiment and it dominated the painter. It made demands on him, for example lightness of palette. It could not suffer darkness. Jacques Émile Blanche describes how Monet would sit watching the sea breaking on the shore at Dieppe, its foam wetting his beard, until darkness drove him away. The dusk, night, the dark naves of cathedrals filled him with fear. Once when he was in the dark, he asked a friend to speak to him and said: "When it is dark, it seems to me as if I were dying, and I can't think any more."

By "I" he meant his own eyesight. Perhaps his love of light was due to the fact that at one time he was in danger of losing his sight, which was saved only by means of an operation. And it was with his eye that he painted, with atoms of coloured splinters. His eye did not worry about the conflict between the creative and the poetic sides of his genius. It sought to achieve mastery in the service of a principle, and it dominated both his tendencies. These it did not need, for it sufficed for it to be allied with taste. With his eye and his taste and the hand of a great virtuoso, Claude Monet created those works which "the world" admired so much, the eight wall-pictures of water-lilies in the Tuileries museum. These pictures have no soul and no heart; nor have they any real poetry; they are too sweet for that. Nevertheless they are remarkably beautiful. Not in the sense of great art, but in the sense of conspicuous ability, not in the sense of the traditions of great painting, but in that of "haute couture", which could draw matchless inspiration for cloths, shawls and hats, sufficient to last for centuries, from the remarkable taste in colour here displayed. They are eminently French, not in the spirit of Notre-Dame or the Faubourg Saint-Germain, but in the sense of the 16th Arrondissement. They might form incomparable models for the mural decoration of salons and drawing-rooms.

There is no doubt that Impressionism brought with it an enrichment of the means available for painting. But this excursion into the open air and the sunlight was a costly undertaking for those who took part in it. Through it Manet lost the crown of his genius, while Monet, Pissarro and Sisley, each to a greater or less degree, sacrificed the possibility of further developing their great gifts. Only one man came out of the experiment with a whole skin, and that was Auguste Renoir.

His life, which lasted from 1841 to 1919, began in the modest middle-class surroundings of a small craftsman, and ended in the world-wide glory of a great artist. It was an exceptionally happy one. Certainly he must have had his bad as well as his good times, but he passed through both with the same equanimity. His life was like that of a tree or a flower, without any of the complications which men bring to nature. He developed in its midst without difficulty and absorbed himself in it without sacrificing the essential factors of his character. His life was a natural and simple process, undisturbed by intellectual, philosophical or theoretical considerations. His problems were limited to the field of his profession. He had the symmetry, the tranquillity and the naturalness which animals and flowers possess to a higher degree than men. There were no conflicts in his soul and no room for tragic events. He was by nature an optimist and an eroticist in a wide and good sense. Flowers, fruit and women were for him a lasting source of gentle and pleasurable excitement. In addition to this he was at one and the same time a gourmet and a gourmand. But "moderation" always ruled him.

Spiritually he was remarkably sound and balanced. His equilibrium was never threatened by intellectual speculations, nor even by those chance elements which accompany experiments. He never became dependent on anything; he always found his way out again, through the solid richness of his own character. Thus it came about that the claims of Impressionism never lured him into uncertain remoteness; he never strayed far from his studio but always returned home safe and sound. What he painted and how he painted had its roots in his own being. For both something was necessary—a kind of "ideal". The objects he painted—apart from portraits—were naked girls, sunlit landscapes, flowers and fruit. The essential elements of his painting he found in the Louvre, the new method of expression outside in the open air. This was all unequivocal and clear, just as his bourgeois life was ordered and punctual.

In the choice of his subjects we find the revelation of a cheerful, sensual temperament, enjoying the sunny side of life, youth, spring and summer. In individual cases he was not hard to please. To him all young girls were alike, just as all flowers and fruit are alike. They might, as he said to Vollard, have " dirt on their behinds ", but that did not matter so long as their skins were susceptible to sunshine. He may have painted fifty or a hundred thousand pounds too much of human flesh in his life (and on account of the invariability of the types this is apt to get on our nerves, especially as not all the pictures are good), but he did not do this merely because he was aware that whoever possesses the " sentiment des tétons et des fesses " and makes good use of it in painting is a made man. On the contrary it was because he was obliged to go on painting like that. For him it was a part of life, as necessary as breathing.

He did not like the Mona Lisa, for he said that a stream running through grass was worth more than her smile. Nevertheless the popularity of his pictures, like that of Leonardo's, is primarily based on the values of erotic sentiment and expression. The artist who paints an " Olympia " estranges the public. Renoir's girls delight the senses and are the source of pleasant dreams. It is easy to imagine that their creator was a great painter.

Renoir was in fact a good painter. For in addition to the erotic elements, the artistic values play an important role in his pictures. But not the melodic values which we find in the " Lola ", the " Olympia " or the " Balcony ". In Renoir's character there was an aversion to everything peculiar; he had a tendency to remain always " in the ranks ". He did not aspire to do things better than the Almighty had created them. He had a bourgeois mistrust of everything that led away from nature towards imaginary heights, towards sublimities which cannot be controlled. His keen appreciation of " moderation " did not permit enthusiasm for the unusual. He was closer to Mozart than to Bach. His grey tone values, where they are present, are not realized on the highest level. Cézanne's table-cloths are of finer texture than his girls' bath-towels, which in general are of about the same quality as the dress of David's Madame Récamier. Usually he prefers not to take advantage of the opportunities of introducing grey tone values into his pictures, and uses white and grey as colours, associating them with the other colours of the picture. In the same way Delacroix, in his " Algerian Women ", not only missed the opportunity of a magnificent harmonic effect afforded by the brown of the negress and the grey of the short sleeve, but also limited himself to two colours in the grey tone of the sleeve itself—colours which do not call forth our enthusiasm either singly or together. The Delacroix who inspired Renoir was not Manet's great and severe model, but one who accorded with the other gods he worshipped—with Veronese, Rubens, Boucher and Watteau. And also with Diaz, whose pupil Renoir felt himself to be. When he was twenty years old (he had already left behind him the stages of artisanship, the painting of porcelain, fans and curtains), he met Diaz in Fontainebleau, and Diaz showed him how to paint in the open air. Later he made the acquaintance of Manet, who taught him lightness of palette, while Monet introduced him to sunshine and the art of disintegrating colours.

" One could sum up the career of Renoir ", wrote Roger-Marx, " by saying that he started as a flower and gradually developed into the fruit." This metaphor reminds me of works of his which used to be together in collections but are now scattered all over the world, and of others which have remained in museums or in permanent private possession. In " Mère Anthony's Cabaret ", painted in 1866, which I myself do not remember, the bud is still tightly closed. But the " Lisa " in the Folkwang Museum, painted one year later, reveals with its raw grandeur the growth of the green sheath and heralds the imminent bursting forth of the bloom. In the " Grenouillère ", painted in 1868, which I once saw at Durand-Ruel's, the first glimmer of soft light penetrates to the now unresisting leaves. Never, however, have I felt more deeply the unspeakable delight which the perception of the opening bud may signify than when I stood before the picture of a nude boy with a cat in the former Arnhold Collection. The full bloom I learned to admire on seeing the portrait of Madame de Pourtalès, painted in 1870, in the former Schmitz Collection. This picture has the gravity, the pride, the deliberation in giving itself, of a dark-red rose which has just bloomed. Many of the colour values Renoir was able to draw from his close contact with nature: the red of the dress, curtain and chair, the green of the decorations. But the black, his most magnificent colour, the queen of colours as he called it, he drew from his own soul, combining it with grey and red in the curtain to form a harmony of touching beauty. He could paint quite large pictures in black, like the portrait of Madame X in the Louvre, which dates from 1874. I have seen too the light-coloured "Riding Track" —a kind of Maréchal Niel rose—which used to be at Rouart's and is now in the Hamburg Kunsthalle. But among the most beautiful of these early works were two paintings of which I could never see enough when they were in Durand-Ruel's private collection, the celebrated "Loge" and the "Danseuse", both painted in 1874. After this came the prolific period of full bloom with its numerous portraits, beginning with the light one of Monsieur Choquet, now belonging to Oskar Reinhart, and the charming portrait of little Mademoiselle Durand-Ruel, both of which somewhat resemble fruit-blossoms. To the same period belong the pictures of the shore at Wagremont and Berneval and those of the Grands Boulevards, reminding us of the porcelain-like quality of white petals. Then the sunlight of Impressionism penetrated more and more strongly into the calyxes, which opened wider and lost some of their colour. In the celebrated "Moulin de la Galette", the abundance of nuances excludes the individual colours or any combination of clear and visible harmonies. We find instead concentrations of different-coloured groups, which, joined together with neutral fillings, create compositional values giving rhythmical animation to the planes of the picture. The beginning of this process of decay, which consists in the shifting of the point of balance from the sense determined by the artistic values to the organization of the surface, is likewise perceptible in the great work painted in 1881, the "Rowers"—a standard example of Impressionism and one of its most perfect realizations. The mastery of artistic means here displayed and the way in which the atmosphere of a period has been captured, make us forget the decline in the artistic values.

One day the soul of Renoir ceased to blossom, the petals fell to the ground and nothing was left but the bare twigs. This period began in 1883 and lasted five years. He had no longer confidence in this blooming beauty, which gradually lost its form. He became suddenly aware of the dangers of Impressionism, interrupted his excursion into the open air and returned to his studio. He subjected himself to the discipline of line and modelled himself upon Ingres. A characteristic picture of this hard and severe period is his "Young woman suckling her child", painted in 1886. But the blossoming of his soul was destined to bring forth fruit. It developed slowly and we can recognize it in the "Young girl at the piano", painted in 1892, with the still rather harsh colours of immaturity. The process of ripening, of fulfilment, now begins, and is exemplified in the pictures of the former Gagnat Collection, where the incredible vigour of the red and green colour values results in the formation of striking harmonies, filling the room as if with great music. I am reminded too of the "Baigneuse" in the Reinhart Collection, and of the majestic picture painted seven years before the end of this existence which was continually striving upwards: the portrait of Madame de Galéa.

Here Renoir reaches the fullness of his maturity. His strong will-power enabled him to struggle against an illness which ended with the crippling of his hands. From the summit which he had attained he could look back on the valleys where lay the course of his quiet and modest life, his marriage, his children, one or two journeys—to Africa, England, Spain, Italy and Munich—a life which found a peaceful, bourgeois ending in Cagnes near Nice.

Renoir's greatness consists in the gradual ascent of his art, which led him to this termination, to his fulfilment. The latter, however, is based on his intimate connection with nature, which allowed him, far from all human pride, to bring forth flowers and fruit like a humble tree in a field.

Portrait of Richard Wagner. Drawing by Auguste Renoir

Drawing by Édouard Manet

III.

DEGAS · GAUGUIN · LAUTREC

About this time there were one or two painters who cannot be considered as belonging to the Impressionists and who in fact refused to be numbered amongst them. Nevertheless they were to a certain extent connected with Impressionism, even if the relationship was only intermittent and superficial. To this group belongs Edgar Degas, who for several years exhibited his pictures together with those of the other Impressionists and frequented their company at the Café Guerbois. The bond between them was probably the inclination towards experiments, and Degas differed from the others in that inside this sphere of activity he employed other methods. Impressionism had its roots in the natural heartiness of the bourgeoisie, but the standpoint of Degas was the aloof curiosity of the man of good position.

The de Gas family belonged to the old provincial nobility, but it had transferred its activities to the world of business. Edgar's grandfather had founded a bank in Naples and his father was born in that city. There was Italian blood, too, in the family. Vollard describes as follows the appearance of Edgar Degas in his old age: "What an air of distinction emanates from the figure of this poor old man! One might have taken him for one of those men of the distant past, a portrait of the Italian school which had climbed down from its frame. Degas had Italian ancestors, and in his old age he reverted to the Neapolitan type." His mother was a Creole of French descent. The Degas owned a cotton factory in New Orleans.

Edgar Degas was born in Paris in 1834. In 1855 he went to the École des Beaux-Arts and in the following year visited Naples and Rome, where he worked at the Villa Medici and copied drawings by Botticelli, Mantegna, Signorelli and Poussin. Later he copied Holbein's "Anne of Cleves", Giorgione's "Holy Family" and Poussin's "Rape of the Sabines". To his admiration for the last-named artist was soon added an interest in David and a great reverence for Ingres, who was nearer to him than any other painter. We must not forget to mention the Japanese artists Outamaro and Hokusai, so that the list of artists who were of importance in the development of his artistic individuality reads as follows: the above-named Quattrocentisti and Ingres for line, Poussin for movement, and the two Japanese for distribution according to volume instead of according to surface. The values of movement, space and composition under the domination of line became the formula which determined the essential character of his art.

The reader may ask how the purely artistic values fared in the presence of these other values which we are accustomed to call "plastic". The psychological factors in the character of Degas himself will help us to solve this problem. His most prominent characteristics were timidity, bashfulness and pride. These made him reserved in his dealings with other people, and solitary. He wanted to have as little to do with others as possible. He allowed no one to approach him except one or two friends. He dreaded intimate discussions more than anything else, and to any attempt in that direction he replied with sarcastic observations. Even when Henri Rousseau asked him frankly: "Now, Monsieur Degas, are you pleased with the way the sale is going?" he remained silent and embarrassed. When he was invited to a meal, the dogs had to be concealed and no flowers placed upon the table. He was afraid of both, because they might have induced the other guests to indulge in sentimentalities. Although in his old age he found solitude distressing, he refused to contemplate marriage, fearing that one day his wife might have said of one of his pictures: "What you've done there is really pretty."

How could a man with such a character be expected to broadcast his confessions to the world? And what else but confessions were the great melodic values of Manet and the grey tone values of Corot? Degas turned a Delacroix he had bought with its face to the wall, so that nobody might share his pleasure in the picture. And if he could not even bear to share the confessions of a third party with others, how could he have brought himself to throw his own confessions on to the market? It must be remembered that he was well acquainted with these values and was able to discern their relative importance. "Don't talk to me about 'plein-air'", he said to Vollard. "Poor Manet! After painting his Maximilien and his Christ with the angels, he had to give up those glorious browns to go and paint a picture like his 'Washing Day'." Degas was also familiar with the subject of grey tone values and had a great desire to purchase Corot's magnificent picture of Chartres which now hangs in the Louvre. The creation of such values, however, is based on feeling, and it was not in his nature to betray any. Perhaps the greatest wish of his life was to become a second Ingres, but he did not succeed in realizing even this colder and more remote manner of expressing great artistic convictions.

That he was not without ambition is proved by the large historical pictures with which he made his début. They have something in their character of works executed for the "Prix de Rome". In the interiors, compositions and portraits which make up his work, isolated melodic values of great beauty may be found, and also grey tone values and fine colour values, but on the whole it must be admitted that his pictures, with all their air of distinction, often betray a neutrality devoid of feeling which misses every opportunity of making great artistic confessions.

Thus it came about that this very aristocratic man, sensitive and quick to take offence, who was one of the finest connoisseurs and lovers of the highest values in painting, renounced them all in his own work, just as he banished flowers from his life. He diverted his interest to the "plastic" values, in which he was an innovator and an inventor. The most perfect pictures he created are those in which a rather impersonal, but distinguished attitude is combined with the formation of values of movement, space and composition. His "Place de la Concorde" has always seemed to me a splendid example of this kind.

The essential aim of this long artistic career, so filled with work, was that of giving life to his pictures with the smallest possible expenditure of means, with an intensity which is found before him only in Carpaccio and after him only in one or two still living modern primitives. To this end he endeavoured to capture and retain movements which no one before or after him has noticed (except perhaps Lautrec, who, however, interpreted them subjectively and in accordance with sentiment), movements which seem to us to be transitory but which are nevertheless typical. In addition to this, under the influence of Japanese art, he tried to arrange his surfaces in a new way, independent of formal ideas .(In this respect too something similar is to be found only in Lautrec.)

There is no greater contrast imaginable in painting than that between Renoir and Degas. Whereas the work of the former, obedient to the laws of nature, spontaneously brought forth flowers and fruit, the work of Degas developed in accordance with the strict requirements of an observant and calculating intellect. It was this intellect, and not sensuality as was the case with Renoir, which determined the subjects of his pictures. In his series of racing pictures, dancers, laundresses and women at their toilette, Degas thought that he could make the best use of his knowledge of the plastic values.

Towards the end of the 1870's his interest in these values was so predominant and his regard for the artistic values so attenuated, that he used mainly pastel colours, the beauty of which existed already and did not need to be discovered. In this way he rid himself at one stroke of the responsibility for the great artistic values, and was content to endow the gravity of his plastic problems with an enchanting exterior by using the dusty purple, pink, blue, violet and orange of his crayons. But the butterfly's wings which thus resulted were in reality the outcome of a tragic and painful sacrifice.

Degas had an unlimited contempt for the "art-loving public", and an invincible mistrust of that public's judgements. One may therefore suppose that he adopted a sceptical attitude towards the unparalleled success of his art (his "Danseuses" in the Rouart Collection fetched nearly half a million francs in 1912). His growing aloofness from the society of others must have been further augmented by the consciousness that he had not achieved what he hoped to do and that the crowning glory was lacking in his works. He has enriched painting with several beautiful and unusual works, but the highest achievements at which he aimed are not among them. An eccentric man descended from an old family, he missed, in the midst of his experiments, hesitations and trivialities, the great creative moment, and when he was going blind he must often have tried to gather from the works of Ingres which he collected how far what he had achieved was inferior to what he had set out to do.

His life lost all its savour for him when he was no longer able to work, and he died in 1917.

*

Another artist who must be mentioned here is Paul Gauguin. At Vollard's in the Rue Laffitte, about a year after his death, I saw a large picture by him, one of those beautiful, luxuriant, tranquil figures of Tahiti women, her arms raised to pluck the flowers or fruits of a tree. The effect of colour and attitude was so magnificent—or at least so it seemed to me at that time—that I earnestly desired to become the owner of the picture. Vollard mentioned 2,500 francs as the price, and as I had not this sum at my disposal, I spent unhappy days and nights regretting that I was unable to fulfil my wish. Later on, in a collection which has long ceased to exist, I saw some of his principal Tahiti works, and my admiration, far from diminishing, became greater still.

Since then more than thirty years have passed, during which I have had few opportunities of seeing his works, but a short time ago I visited the Gauguin exhibition which a great Parisian gallery had organized and I was amazed at the level maintained throughout his artistic development. True, not all the most important works of all his periods were represented—Impressionistic Paris, Pont-Aven, Martinique, Tahiti, the Marquesas Islands—but so much that is important and characteristic was there that it sufficed to give a general idea and to remind me of the still greater pictures. But it seemed to me as if the colours had faded and become blacker. Those were not the glorious colours of the South Sea islands, but the dusty scenery of the Châtelet theatre for a Jules Verne performance. Moreover, in these pictures the mountains and houses were of paper, the snow was not snow, the majesty of reality was lacking. Their poetry lay not in the brown, pink, blue, red or yellow, but in the subjects. They were literary pieces painted with unsubstantial materials. In the spatial arrangement it often seemed that everything was in disorder; at one point a tree belonging to the background went on growing in the foreground. In the corners coloured obscurities lay concealed, defying analysis and disturbing in their effect. There were dirty patches and vague attempts at "Stimmung". Here and there a beautiful tree appeared, which had grown up in the garden of Pissarro, a dog which seemed to regret that he had not been painted by Lautrec. And there were green stretches of turf painted in such a manner that one was reminded of the thick fingers of an unattractive hand.

Have we ourselves, or in other words our aesthetic and artistic judgement, changed so much since the beginning of this century, since the days when Wagnerian opera reached its height, or is it the pictures which bear in themselves the germs of decay, so that they disintegrate like the picture of Dorian Gray? Perhaps the answer to both these questions is in the affirmative. It must, however, be recorded that these works of Gauguin have retained all their illustrative beauty. As photographic reproductions they can move us even to-day. We can peruse this "dream-world" with the same pleasure which we take in reproductions of Böcklin's mythological pictures. But when we find ourselves before the originals, the illusion of "greatness" is destroyed by a feeling that they contain something false and bombastic. Gauguin's sculptures have the same effect on us to-day, though at one time we thought them sublime. False and bombastic, too, is the title of one of them: "Be filled with love and you will be happy." Like that of one of his last great paintings: "Whence do we come, what are we, and whither are we going?" That is the keynote of his art, which is reflective, literary and given to moralizing.

When we turn to Gauguin's life, we find that perhaps in him too there was a disproportion between the modest scale of his gifts and his pretensions which were not always on the same scale. When his own will did not share in the decision, fate brought about grotesque disproportions. Born in Paris in 1848, the son of an insignificant journalist, he had before him, in contrast to the narrow circle which bounded his own life, the exotic and luxurious flora of his mother's family, among whom there figured a Spanish colonel and a Viceroy of Peru who lived to be 113 years old. It seems almost like the narrative of a film that the father should die on the way to the wonderful country from which he hoped so much, and the mother and children arrive alone in Lima, where they remained for four years. Then came the return to Orleans and the narrow life of the first years. At seventeen Paul entered the mercantile marine and was still a sailor when the Franco-Prussian war broke out. After that he became a clerk in a bank. In 1873 he married a Danish girl of good family who bore him five children. The stage seemed set for a peaceful middle-class existence, when suddenly he was seized with the desire to paint. As his work at the Bourse kept him busy during the week, he became what was known as a "Sunday painter". He got to know Pissarro and afterwards the other Impressionists, whose pictures he purchased out of his savings. His landscapes at this time were soft and pretty, painted with a timid application of Impressionistic technique. With painting as his "violon d'Ingres" he was now able to lead a modest but happy existence. But he wanted to soar higher still, he gave up his work at the bank and devoted himself entirely to painting. As was only natural, he failed to sell any of his pictures and was consequently without any source of income. In the vain hope that living would be cheaper there, he went to Rouen, and thence to Copenhagen, to his wife's family, who were incapable of understanding either him or his actions. He separated from the mother of his children and returned with his son to Paris, where first the child and then he himself fell ill. Years of misery followed, during which he earned a little money by pasting up posters at railway-stations.

During the following years Gauguin went several times to Brittany, to Pont-Aven and Le Pouldu, where he met Bernard and Serusier; with them he severed his artistic connection with Impressionism, thus becoming the head of a school. There he painted several well-known pictures, such as the "Calvaires" and the "Yellow Christ". In between he visited Panama, in connection with the work on the canal, and Martinique, where the beauty of simple and powerful colours in undivided planes completed his spiritual withdrawal from Impressionism. In 1888 he held his first exhibition, which brought him very little. In the following year the proprietor of a café showed some of Gauguin's works at the international exhibition.

How is it that this man, who went about the Quartier Montparnasse in an astrakhan cap, like a "magnificent and gigantic Magyar", carrying a walking-stick which he had carved himself, makes so little appeal to our sympathy despite the obvious earnestness of his attachment to art? How is it that we feel so little emotion at the thought that he sacrificed his wife and children, his tranquillity and his well-being, to devote himself to painting? That we feel less pity for his poverty than for that of Pissarro, Monet and Sisley? That while our hearts ache when we think of the material and spiritual misery of Van Gogh and his madness, yet the sorrows and conflicts of the likewise unbalanced Gauguin leave us unmoved? It is perhaps because, rightly or wrongly, we see in him the predecessor of a generation of Montparnasse painters who, eccentric in their attire and sterile in their ideas, maintain that they do not paint, but "it" paints through them. Because his pose, his strivings and his claims are out of all proportion to the modest facts of his material and spiritual existence.

At this time Gauguin gained two friends and admirers: Charles Morice, who wrote a good book about him, and Daniel de Monfreid, who became the faithful administrator of Gauguin's affairs while he was in Tahiti. An auction of thirty pictures which brought in nearly ten thousand francs enabled him to undertake the long journey. Disappointed with Papeete, the capital, where life is but a miserable caricature of life in Europe, he moved to another place, lived with the natives, painted several of his most famous pictures, executed sculptures and wrote "Noa Noa", in which, in reality, he describes life on the island as it might have been, not as it really is, for it consists mainly of disease and poverty.

From an uncle in Orleans Gauguin inherited some property and was able to exhibit at Durand-Ruel's forty pictures, of which eleven were sold. He appeared in a long blue coat with mother-of-pearl buttons, and a waistcoat fastened at the side; he wore a collar of many colours, a grey felt hat, with a sky-blue band, and white gloves, and carried in one hand a stick adorned with barbaric carvings and a pearl. He lived with a Javanese girl in the midst of exotic objects, in a studio in a house near Montparnasse which no longer exists. When I was young, I myself inhabited this gloomy house in the dark and narrow Rue Vercingétorix—which, by an ironical coincidence, is near the Rue de la Gaîté and in the "Plaisance" quarter—and lived there long enough to realize how grotesque must have been the contrast between this bourgeois milieu of modest families and the theatrical and Bohemian appearance of Gauguin.

In 1894 he went to Copenhagen, where he definitely broke with his wife. The Javanese girl accompanied him to Brittany, where he fell ill; she returned alone to Paris, stole the contents of the studio and vanished. Although an auction of his pictures in the following year brought him only a meagre result, Gauguin, relying on the promises of his friends, decided to make a second journey to Tahiti. There he painted his most characteristic pictures—fantastic compositions and landscapes with pink roads. He painted in spite of illness and lack of money, which were responsible for his making an attempt on his life. His letters to Monfreid show that he was in the depths of despair. His friends in Paris, as so often happens in life, left him in the lurch, and his only consolation was his connection with Vollard, which had just begun. He had trouble with the authorities and in 1901 moved to the Marquesas Islands, where he went on working. He sent pictures to Paris and his life seemed to be becoming more tranquil. Then in 1903 he had a quarrel with a gendarme and was sentenced by the court of primary jurisdiction to three months' imprisonment and a fine of one thousand francs. The case was never brought before the court of appeal, for he died before it could be heard.

The almost ridiculous amount of misfortune, sickness and poverty which afflicted him during his lifetime moves us to the same sorrow which we feel for every suffering, striving man; but we cannot feel that his life was tragic enough to arouse our deeper emotions. We are hindered by the fact that he created too many indifferent works as well as the beautiful works which retain their place in our memory, that he was too calculating in his despairing letters, that his bombastic exterior contained too little human and artistic substance, that this "head of a school" contributed nothing either to the treasure-house of the great general values in painting or to that of the particular values to be found in French tradition, and that his gifts were not adequate to justify an independent and solitary existence outside these artistic circles.

*

What nature denied to Gauguin, another artist, likewise connected with Impressionism, possessed to a very high degree. Henri de Toulouse-Lautrec-Monfa had breeding. An offshoot of the old family of the Counts of Toulouse, his character had a genuineness which was able to dispense with the make-up of eccentric costumes and grotesque walking-sticks, a natural straightforwardness which rejected the hocus-pocus of a paradise full of almond-eyed damsels languorously stretching their arms towards banana trees. Lautrec's paradise was the "Moulin Rouge", peopled by ladies like "Goulue" and her kind, whose hands were accustomed to very different gestures. It was Montmartre, not Montparnasse. His ancestry was such that even the most unusual happenings produced a natural effect on him and never became "chiqué". His father was one of the last great gentlemen who still practised falconry. When the father was in Paris, he rode in the Bois on a mare, whom he milked when he was thirsty, eating a few rolls with the milk. If he was dissatisfied with the laundress, he washed his own socks in the gutter before his house. He brought a swarm of bees with him from the country and allowed them to fly about the room. The Comtesse de Toulouse-Lautrec was a refined, reserved woman who knew Latin. She was a close relation of her husband, and thus it came about that their son was born deformed. "S'il vous plaît, Monsieur le Comte", said a tailor who wanted to measure him, pointing to a step-ladder. And once at Maxim's, when Lautrec rose and left his pencil on the table, somebody called out after him: "Monsieur, you have forgotten your walking-stick." He used to say of himself that he was "only a half-bottle". Let us add, however, that his intellect and his soul filled it completely and the contents were genuine and of the finest quality.

He was born at Albi in 1864, and came to Paris in 1883, working at first in the studios of Bonnat and Cormon. Not for long, however. He lived in Montmartre, near the establishments from which he was to draw so much inspiration, and later moved to the Rue Frochot. From there it was not far to the "Moulin Rouge", where there was a table reserved for him and where there was dancing in the evening. Among the dancers were "Goulue", "Jane Avril", "Grille d'égout", "Eglantine", "Nini-Patte-en-l'air" and "Valentin le désossé". Quite close to his house was the "Rat mort", the most interesting "boîte" in the Place Pigalle. Diagonally opposite lay the "Hanneton" with its red shutters, frequented by women together, some of them wearing men's evening-dress, with eyeglasses and high boots, and carrying little whips. Palmyr, who had a face like a bulldog and a hoarse voice like a carter, had a bar not far off. Then there was the café in the Place Blanche, and higher up the Moulin de la Galette, where the little employés used to dance with quite small girls. Lautrec's stumpy figure appeared in all these places, in the company of his unusually tall cousin Tapié de Celeyran. The curious couple also used to show themselves in the neighbourhood of the Boulevards, at Maxim's or the Bar Achille, a meeting-place of clowns, jockeys and trainers. When this bar shut, they went on to Weber's, where Jean de Tinan, Moréas and Léon Daudet were wont to meet, where Marcel Proust might occasionally appear, or the burly figure of Sebastian Melmoth, once known to fame as Oscar Wilde. They also visited the houses of ill-fame, where they made friends with the girls, who confided to them all the comic and tragic details of their lives of slavery. The great evenings were when Yvette Guilbert appeared, with her long neck and the long black gloves on her thin arms, singing her "voyou" songs in a marvellous voice. Such evenings they considered to be consecrated to art, whereas their visits to the Comédie Française were merely a source of amusement, owing to the comic pathos of the actors and the solemnity of the old-fashioned audience. Even this did not exhaust the list of Lautrec's favourite resorts. There was also the circus, where he was interested in the clowns and the "haut manège", the Buffalo racing-track where he admired the athletes, and the Jardin des Plantes, where he made friends with the animals.

Such was Toulouse-Lautrec's world. He lived in it and his artistic genius glorified it. Numerous paintings, drawings, lithographs and posters were created by his hand, with all the personalities of this artificial and separate world as subjects: dancers from whose mask-like faces the harsh light eliminates every trace of humanity; old viveurs whose thoughts and feelings have withered and who move about like marionettes; women who have passed through every stage of vice and perversion and, deformed both physically and morally, have developed into an extraordinary and incredible branch of the human species, with terrifying tics and convulsions, puzzling reactions and unusual gestures; jockeys with bandy legs like Lautrec's own; athletes with large faces and small heads; actors whose ridiculous appearance in the disfiguring glare of the footlights contrasted with the dignity of their roles; prostitutes who went through the repulsive details of the "before" and "after" with the same dull innocence with which a middle-class girl darns a stocking.

This man of good breeding who had been born a dwarf, who had the soul of a sportsman and yet was so weak on his legs that he had to drive everywhere in fiacres, loved this world of eccentrics and unfortunates, whom he depicted without sentimentality and without caricaturing them. He loved and depicted their facial expressions and their movements. Values of expression and movement constitute the inexhaustible richness of his work. The former not in the sense of the smiling Mona Lisa, that is to say the distinguished and attractive elements, but in the diametrically opposite sense of shamelessness and viciousness. Values of movement not in the sense of those sublime and sweeping gestures with which the figures in the Louvre are worshipped, crowned or buried, but those of neurotics and the stiff movements of the blasés. Colour values exist in these works only for the purpose of emphasizing the values of expression. They are in the service of his immensely suggestive draughtsmanship. They are derived not from the sensual charm of the material, but from the symbolic force of the absinthe-drinkers, the diseased, dead or dying figures who possessed it. If harmonic values occur, consisting perhaps of salmon-pink, green and ivory yellow, they are only accidental. These colours were born under the light of electric lamps and are strangers to those which the Impressionists discovered in the sunlight.

Spiritually Lautrec had nothing to do with the Impressionists. He did not like landscapes. Walking was out of the question for him. Water in his opinion was useful for washing in or for shooting wild-duck on. But his favourite exercise was rowing in his studio on a specially constructed apparatus. The only thing that interested him in Impressionistic painting was the technique. The application of coloured strokes allowed him to avoid unequivocal decisions as to colour, which usually require the distribution of colour into large patches. The former system was better adapted to the secondary role of an almost literary auxiliary, which was what colour meant for him. Only later, when he had mastered his art, could he dispense with Impressionistic technique. It is easy to understand that he was nearer to Degas than to the Impressionists and that he submitted to his influence. Speaking of influences, that of the Japanese must not be forgotten, to whom he owes those surprising and spirited compositional values which have nothing to do with the classical ideals of balance, rhythm and surface.

The life of Toulouse-Lautrec was a short one, his interests were confined within narrow limits, and the artistic values in his pictures were few in number, but his work within its framework was nevertheless raised by deep feeling and remarkable gifts to a pinnacle of genuineness and perfection which will ensure for it a permanent place in the history of art.

Lautrec drank a great deal during his lifetime, but life itself prepared for him the mortal draught, compounded of disease, alcohol and excess. He succumbed to it in 1901, at the age of thirty-eight, in a château belonging to his family.

His father had not been able to look after him, as he was busy shooting. At the time of his son's death he had hurt his foot, and had to follow the funeral procession on horseback.

Drawing by Edgar Degas

THE PLATES

The plates illustrating this volume were selected by Ludwig Goldscheider, who also supervised the work of reproduction

5. ÉDOUARD MANET: THE PICNIC

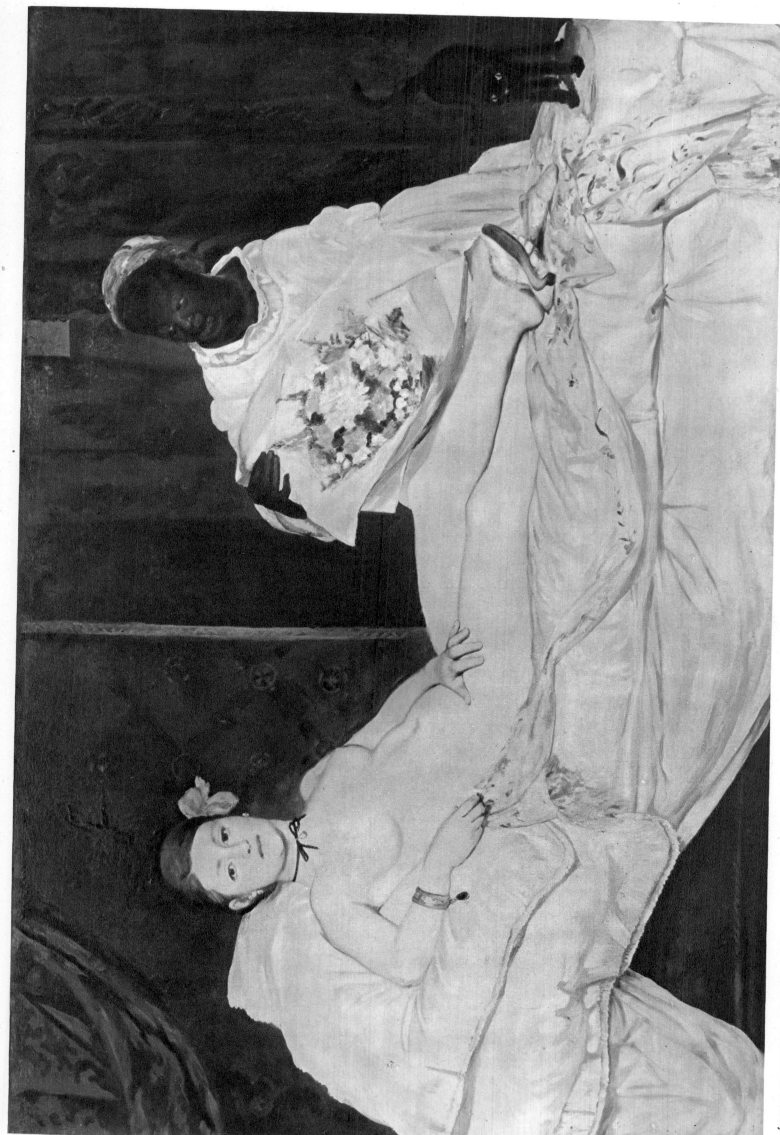

Imp. 2

6. ÉDOUARD MANET: OLYMPIA

MANET. L'ARTISTE (ACTRESS)

8. ÉDOUARD MANET: BULL-FIGHT

9. ÉDOUARD MANET: ANGÉLINE

10. ÉDOUARD MANET: THE PIPER

11. ÉDOUARD MANET: PORTRAIT OF THÉODORE DURET

12. ÉDOUARD MANET: MAN PEELING PEARS (PORTRAIT OF LÉON LEENHOFF)

13. ÉDOUARD MANET: PORTRAIT OF ÉMILE ZOLA

ÉDOUARD MANET. DEPARTURE OF THE STEAMER ("LE DÉPART DU BATEAU DE FOLKESTONE")

15. ÉDOUARD MANET: WHITE PEONIES

16. ÉDOUARD MANET: EXECUTION OF THE EMPEROR MAXIMILIAN OF MEXICO

Imp. 4

17. ÉDOUARD MANET: THE BALCONY

18. ÉDOUARD MANET: LADY WITH FAN (PORTRAIT OF BERTHE MORISOT)

19. ÉDOUARD MANET: MARINE LANDSCAPE ("MARINE A ARCACHON")

21. ÉDOUARD MANET: THE GAME OF CROQUET

23. ÉDOUARD MANET: PORTRAIT OF STÉPHANE MALLARMÉ

24. ÉDOUARD MANET: WASHING DAY ("LE LINGE")

25. ÉDOUARD MANET: AT THE CAFÉ CONCERT

26. ÉDOUARD MANET: THE PARISIENNE (PORTRAIT OF MADAME HÉLÈNE ANDRÉE

27. ÉDOUARD MANET: THE ARTIST (PORTRAIT OF THE PAINTER MARCELLIN DESBOUTINS)

28. ÉDOUARD MANET: NANA

29. ÉDOUARD MANET: FAURE AS HAMLET

30. ÉDOUARD MANET: MADAME MANET ON A SOFA. PASTEL

31. ÉDOUARD MANET: AT THE CAFÉ

35. ÉDOUARD MANET: PORTRAIT OF ANTONIN PROUST

36. ÉDOUARD MANET: YOUNG COUPLE AT LUNCH ("CHEZ LE PÈRE LATHUILLE")

37. ÉDOUARD MANET: IN THE GREENHOUSE

38. ÉDOUARD MANET: THE LION-HUNTER (PORTRAIT OF PERTUISET)

39. ÉDOUARD MANET: PORTRAIT OF HENRI ROCHEFORT

40. ÉDOUARD MANET: MÉRY ("L'AUTOMNE")

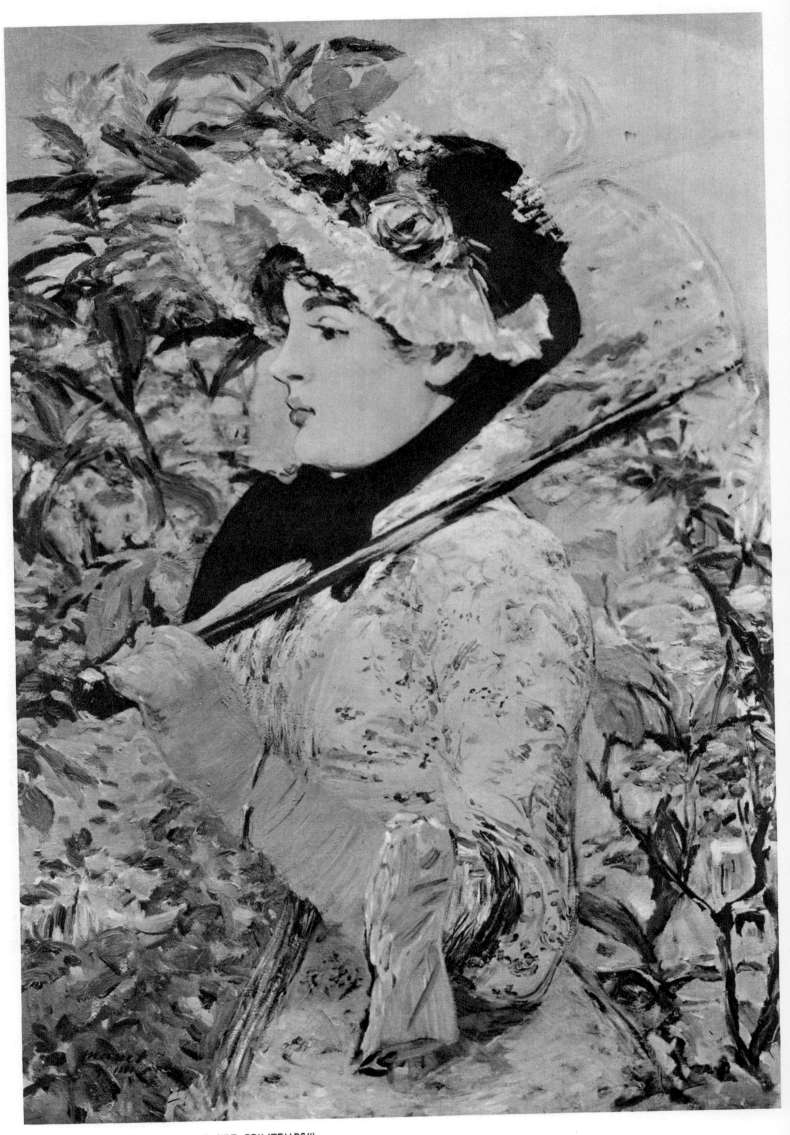

41. ÉDOUARD MANET: JEANNE ("LE PRINTEMPS")

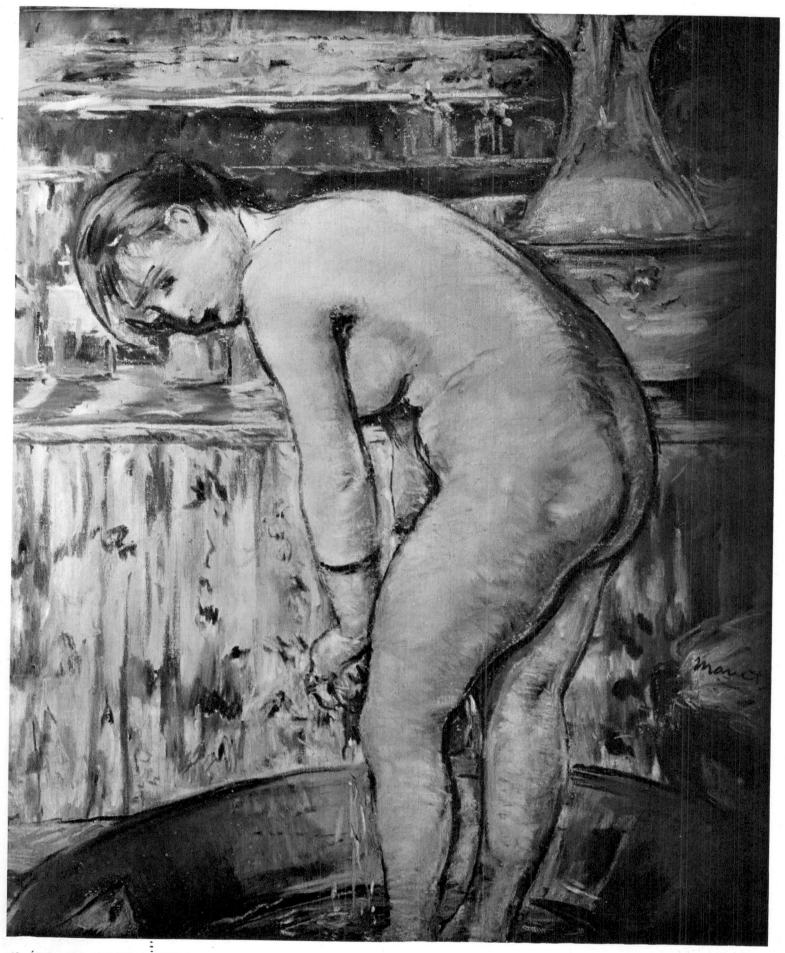

42. ÉDOUARD MANET: BATHERS. PASTEL

44. ÉDOUARD MANET: BAR AT THE FOLIES-BERGÈRE

45. EVA GONZALÈS: BY THE WATER

46. BERTHE MORISOT: A SUMMER'S DAY ("JOUR D'ÉTÉ")

c.Pissarro. 1891

47. CAMILLE PISSARRO: WOMEN GATHERING APPLES. PASTEL

48. CAMILLE PISSARRO: VIEW OF ROUEN ("LA RUE DE L'ÉPICERIE")

50. CAMILLE PISSARRO: THE BOULEVARD DES ITALIENS AT NIGHT

51. CAMILLE PISSARRO: HOUSES IN THE COUNTRY NEAR PARIS

Imp. 8

53. CAMILLE PISSARRO: THE AVENUE DE L'OPÉRA, PARIS ("SOLEIL MATINÉE L'AUTOMNE")

51. ALFRED SISLEY. A CORNER IN A VILLAGE

55. ALFRED SISLEY: SEINE LANDSCAPE

56. ALFRED SISLEY: FLOODS AT PORT-MARLY

57. ALFRED SISLEY: BRIDGE NEAR ARGENTEUIL

58. CLAUDE MONET: THE CHURCH OF SAINT-GERMAIN-L'AUXERROIS, PARIS

9*

59. CLAUDE MONET: FISHERMEN ON THE SEINE NEAR POISSY

60. CLAUDE MONET: THE BRIDGE OVER THE SEINE AT ARGENTEUIL

61. CLAUDE MONET: THE GARE SAINT-LAZARE, PARIS

62. CLAUDE MONET: THE LUNCH

63. CLAUDE MONET: MADAME MONET ON A GARDEN SEAT ("DAME ASSISE DANS UNE PARC")

64. CLAUDE MONET: WATERLOO BRIDGE, LONDON

65. CLAUDE MONET: ANTIBES

66. CLAUDE MONET: ROUEN CATHEDRAL

67. CLAUDE MONET: WOMEN IN A GARDEN

68. CLAUDE MONET: BRIDGE OVER A POOL OF POND LILIES

70. PIERRE-AUGUSTE RENOIR: THE BATHING-PLACE ("LA GRENOUILLÈRE")

71. PIERRE-AUGUSTE RENOIR: LISE

72. PIERRE-AUGUSTE RENOIR: THE PAINTER SISLEY AND HIS WIFE

73. PIERRE-AUGUSTE RENOIR: PORTRAIT OF MONSIEUR CHOCQUET

74. PIERRE-AUGUSTE RENOIR: LADY TAKING TEA

75. PIERRE-AUGUSTE RENOIR: MADAME CHARPENTIER AND HER CHILDREN

76. PIERRE-AUGUSTE RENOIR: ROWERS AT LUNCH

77. PIERRE-AUGUSTE RENOIR: UMBRELLAS

78. PIERRE-AUGUSTE RENOIR: MOTHER AND CHILD (MADAME RENOIR AND HER SON PIERRE)

79. PIERRE-AUGUSTE RENOIR: YOUNG WOMAN WITH FAN

80. PIERRE-AUGUSTE RENOIR: BLONDE GIRL

81. PIERRE-AUGUSTE RENOIR: LA LOGE

82. PIERRE-AUGUSTE RENOIR: THE SWING

83. PIERRE-AUGUSTE RENOIR: LANDSCAPE WITH VIEW OF THE SACRÉ-COEUR, PARIS

THE EDGE OF THE FOREST

85. PIERRE-AUGUSTE RENOIR: WASHERWOMEN

12°

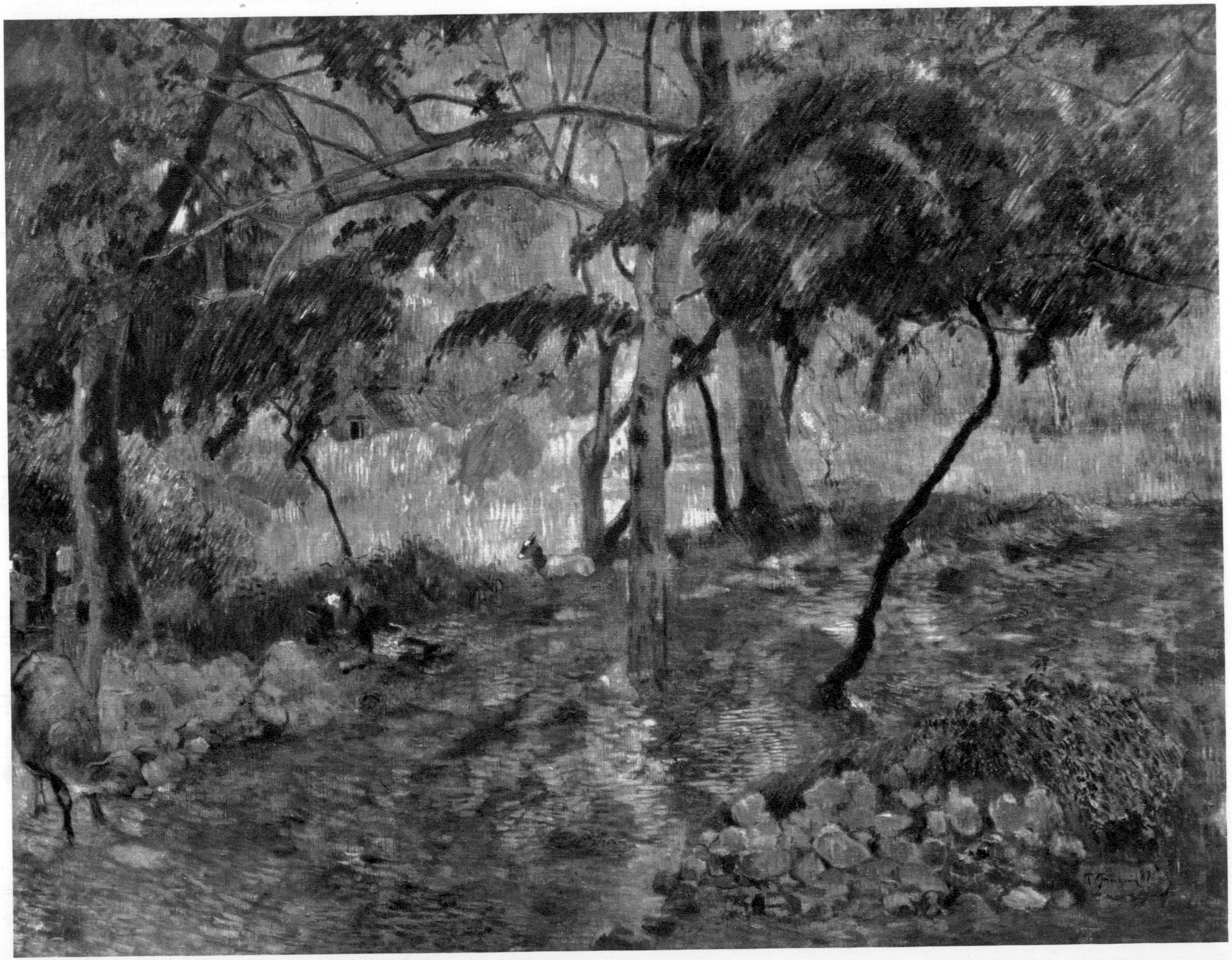

86. PAUL GAUGUIN: TROPICAL LANDSCAPE (MARTINIQUE)

87. PAUL GAUGUIN: HORSEMEN ON THE SHORE

88. PAUL GAUGUIN: WINTER LANDSCAPE

13*

92. PAUL GAUGUIN: PORTRAIT OF VINCENT VAN GOGH

93. PAUL GAUGUIN: SELF-PORTRAIT

94. PAUL GAUGUIN: PORTRAIT OF AN OLD PEASANT

96. EDGAR HILAIRE GERMAIN DEGAS: AT THE RACES

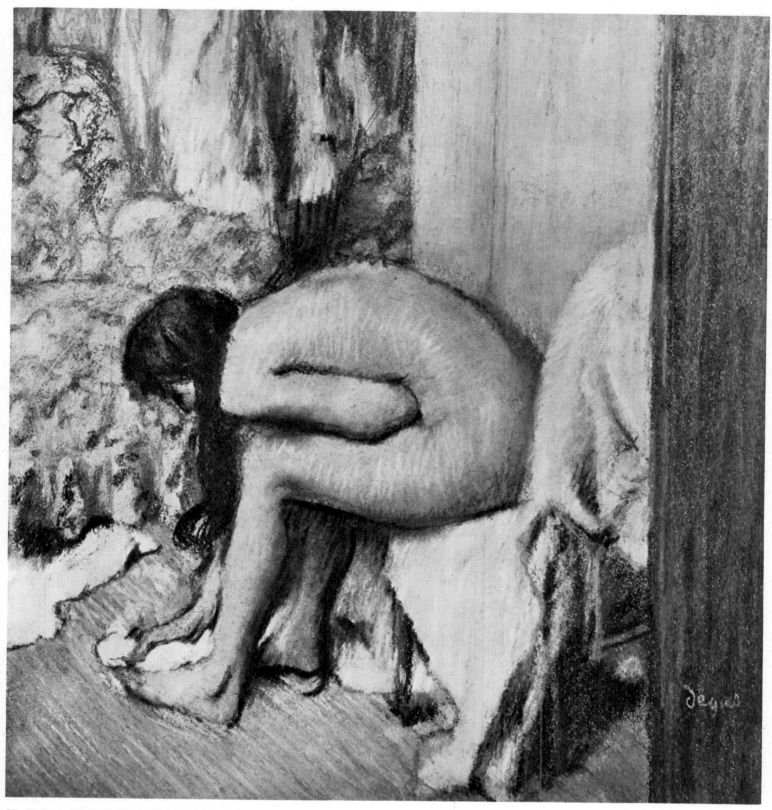

97. EDGAR HILAIRE GERMAIN DEGAS: AFTER THE BATH. PASTEL

98. EDGAR HILAIRE GERMAIN DEGAS: PORTRAIT OF THE DUKE AND DUCHESS OF MORBILI

99. EDGAR HILAIRE GERMAIN DEGAS: AT THE EXCHANGE (PORTRAIT OF MR. ERNEST MAY)

100. EDGAR HILAIRE GERMAIN DEGAS: TWO DANSEUSES. PASTEL

101. EDGAR HILAIRE GERMAIN DEGAS: MISS LOLA AT THE CIRCUS FERNANDO

102. EDGAR HILAIRE GERMAIN DEGAS: CARLO PELLEGRINI, "APE" OF VANITY FAIR

103. EDGAR HILAIRE GERMAIN DEGAS: LADY WITH OPERA-GLASS

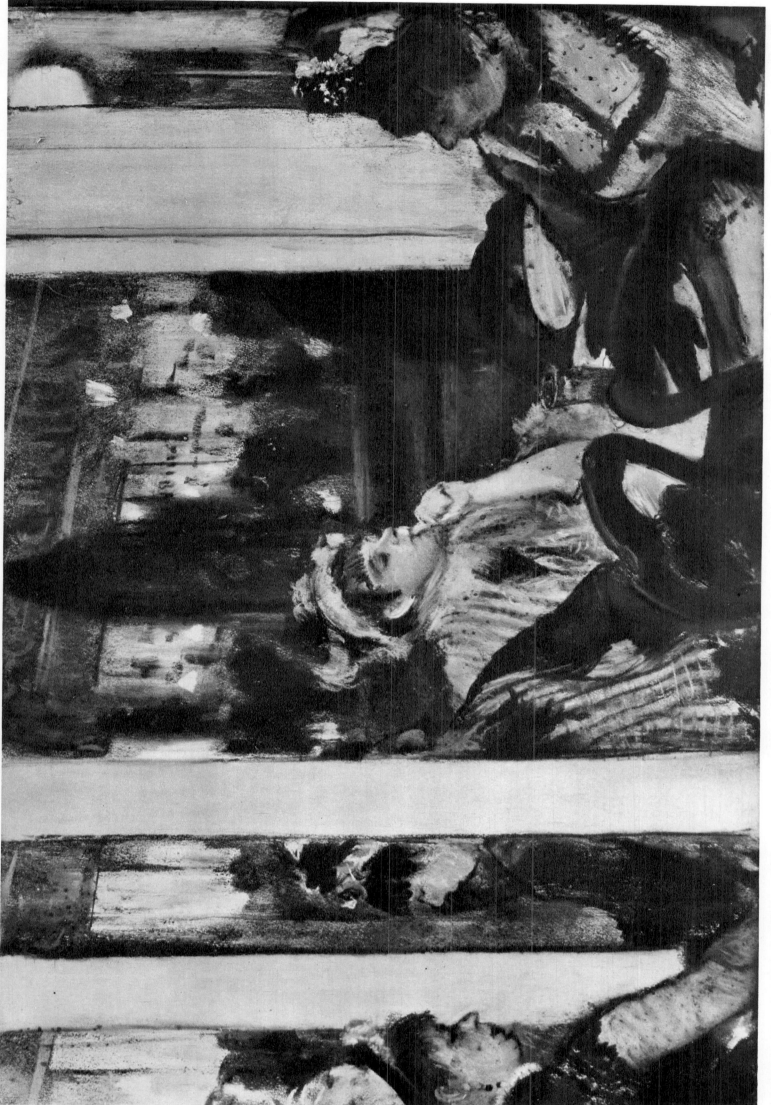

105. EDGAR HILAIRE GERMAIN DEGAS: CAFÉ ON THE BOULEVARD MONTMARTRE. PASTEL

106. EDGAR HILAIRE GERMAIN DEGAS: ABSINTHE (PORTRAIT OF HÉLÈNE ANDRÉE AND MARCELLIN DESBOUTIN)

107. HENRI DE TOULOUSE-LAUTREC: AT THE RESTAURANT (PORTRAIT OF M. BOILEAU)

108. HENRI DE TOULOUSE-LAUTREC: "GOULUE" AND HER SISTER AT THE MOULIN ROUGE

109. HENRI DE TOULOUSE-LAUTREC: PORTRAIT

110. HENRI DE TOULOUSE-LAUTREC: WOMAN, CUTTING HER NAILS

112. HENRI DE TOULOUSE-LAUTREC: PORTRAIT OF M. DE LAURADOUR

113. HENRI DE TOULOUSE-LAUTREC: YOUNG GIRL IN A STUDIO

114. HENRI DE TOULOUSE-LAUTREC: HARLOT ("ROSE LA ROUGE")

115. HENRI DE TOULOUSE-LAUTREC: WOMAN WITH A BLACK BOA

116. HENRI DE TOULOUSE-LAUTREC: MISS MAY BELFORT

117. HENRI DE TOULOUSE-LAUTREC: PROMENADE AT THE MOULIN ROUGE ("LA GOULUE")

LIST OF PLATES

Paintings of which the titles are printed in capitals are reproduced in colour.

ÉDOUARD MANET (1832-1883)

1. Youthful Portrait of Antonin Proust. 1856. 22¹/₁₆×18¹/₂ inches. Tcheco-Slovakia, Private Collection.
2. The Absinthe Drinker. 1859. 51³/₁₆×39 inches. Paris, Durand-Ruel.
3. Lola de Valence. 1862. 48⁹/₁₆×36¹/₄ inches. Paris, Louvre.
4. Concert in the Tuileries Gardens ("La Musique aux Tuileries"). 1862. 29×46 inches. London, Tate Gallery.
5. THE PICNIC ("Le déjeuner sur l'herbe"). 1863. 84¹/₄×106⁵/₈ inches. Paris, Louvre.
6. Olympia. 1863. 51³/₁₆×74¹⁵/₁₆ inches. Paris, Louvre.
7. Baudelaire's Mistress. 1862. 44¹/₂×33¹/₂ inches. Budapest, Museum of Fine Arts.
8. Bull-fight. 1866. 34⁵/₈×43⁵/₁₆ inches. Paris, Durand-Ruel.
9. Angéline. 1865. 35¹³/₁₆×36¹/₄ inches. Paris, Louvre.
10. THE PIPER. 1866. 63¹/₄×38³/₁₆ inches. Paris, Louvre.
11. Portrait of Théodore Duret. 1867. 16¹⁵/₁₆×13³/₄ inches. Paris, Petit Palais.
12. Man peeling pears (Portrait of Léon Leenhoff). About 1868. 33¹/₂×27¹⁵/₁₆ inches. Stockholm, National Museum.
13. Portrait of Émile Zola. 1868. 57¹/₄×43⁵/₁₆ inches. Paris, Louvre.
14. Departure of the Steamer ("Le départ du bateau de Folkestone"). 1869. 23¹/₄×24 inches. Philadelphia, C. S. Tyson Collection.
15. WHITE PEONIES. About 1864. 12¹/₈×18⁵/₁₆ inches. Paris, Louvre.
16. Execution of the Emperor Maximilien of Mexico. About 1868. 99¹/₄×120¹/₄ inches. Mannheim, Kunsthalle.
17. The Balcony. 1869. 66¹/₂×48⁷/₁₆ inches. Paris, Louvre.
18. Lady with fan (Portrait of Berthe Morisot). 1872. 22¹³/₁₆×16¹⁵/₁₆ inches. Paris, Louvre.
19. Marine Landscape ("Marine à Arcachon"). 1871. 9⁷/₁₆×16¹/₂ inches. Paris, Bignou Collection.
20. THE BOAT (Claude Monet and his wife). 1874. 31¹/₂×39 inches. Munich, Neue Staatsgalerie.
21. The Game of Croquet. 1873. 28⁹/₁₆×41³/₄ inches. Frankfurt am Main, Städelsches Kunstinstitut.
22. In a Boat. 1874. 38¹/₄×51¹/₄ inches. New York, Metropolitan Museum.
23. Portrait of Stéphane Mallarmé. 1876. 10¹/₄×13³/₈ inches. Paris, Louvre.
24. Washing Day ("Le linge"). 1874. 57¹/₄×45¹/₄ inches. Berlin, Paul Cassirer.
25. At the Café Concert. 1874. 18¹/₈×15 inches. Baltimore, Walters Collection.
26. The Parisienne (Portrait of Madame Hélène Andrée). About 1875. 75⁵/₈×49¹/₄ inches. Stockholm, National Museum.
27. The Artist (Portrait of the painter Marcellin Desboutin). 1875. 75⁵/₈×50³/₈ inches. Berlin, Arnhold Collection.
28. Nana. 1877. 60⁵/₈×45¹/₄ inches. Hamburg, Kunsthalle.
29. Faure as Hamlet. 1877. 77³/₁₆×50³/₄ inches. Hamburg, Kunsthalle.
30. Madame Manet on a sofa. Pastel. 1878. 19⁵/₈×23⁵/₈ inches. Paris, Louvre.
31. At the Café. 1878. 30⁵/₁₆×32¹¹/₁₆ inches. Berlin, M. Scharf.
32. Road-menders in the Rue de Berne. 1879. 25⁵/₈×31¹/₈ inches. Berlin, Paul Cassirer.
33. George Moore at a café. 1879. 25⁵/₈×31¹/₈ inches. Paris, Albert S. Henraux Collection.
34. Portrait of George Moore. Pastel. 1879. 21³/₄×13⁷/₈ inches. New York, Metropolitan Museum.
35. Portrait of Antonin Proust. 1880. 51⁹/₁₆×38³/₁₆ inches. Toledo, Ohio, U.S.A., Museum of Art.
36. Young Couple at lunch ("Chez le père Lathuille"). 1879. 36¹/₄×44¹/₄ inches. Tournai, Museum.
37. IN THE GREENHOUSE ("La Serre". — Portrait of the painter Guillemet and his wife). 1879. 45¹/₄×59¹/₁₆ inches. Berlin, Nationalgalerie.
38. The Lion-hunter (Portrait of Pertuiset). 1881. 59¹/₁₆×66¹⁵/₁₆ inches. Breslau, Silberberg Collection.
39. Portrait of Henri Rochefort. 1881. 32¹/₄×26³/₁₆ inches. Hamburg, Kunsthalle.
40. Méry Laurent ("L'Automne"). 1882. 29¹/₄×20¹/₁₆ inches. Nancy, Museum of Fine Arts.
41. Jeanne Demasy ("Le Printemps"). 1881. 29¹/₄×20¹/₁₆ inches. New York, Collection of Mrs. Payne-Bingham (on loan to the Metropolitan Museum, New York).
42. Bathers. Pastel. About 1881. Paris, Bernheim Jeune.
43. Manet's country house at Rueil. 1882. 27³/₁₆×35⁷/₁₆ inches. Berlin, Nationalgalerie.
44. Bar at the Folies-Bergère. 1882. 37¹/₂×50 inches. London, Courtauld Institute of Art (on loan to the National Gallery).

EVA GONZALÈS (1850-1883)

45. By the Water. About 1875. 12³/₁₆×13³/₄ inches. Vienna, Belvedere.

BERTHE MORISOT (1841-1895)

46. A Summer's Day ("Jour d'Été"). 17¹/₂×29 inches. London, Tate Gallery.

92. Portrait of Vincent Van Gogh. About 1888. 18 1/8 × 20 7/8 inches. Amsterdam, Gemeente Museum.
93. Self-portrait. London, Wildenstein & Co.
94. Portrait of an old Peasant. Paris, Bernheim Jeune.

EDGAR HILAIRE GERMAIN DEGAS
(1834-1917)

95. The Place de la Concorde, Paris (Portrait of Comte Lepic and his daughter). 1873/74. 31 1/8 × 46 7/16 inches. Berlin, O. Gerstenberg.
96. AT THE RACES. About 1879. 26 1/4 × 32 1/4 inches. Paris, Louvre.
97. After the Bath. Pastel. 1886. Paris, Louvre.
98. Portrait of the Duke and Duchess of Morbili. About 1870. 45 11/16 × 35 1/4 inches. Boston, Museum of Fine Arts.
99. At the Exchange (Portrait of Mr. Ernest May). 39 1/4 × 32 1/3 inches. Paris, Louvre.
100. Two Danseuses. Pastel. About 1874. 37 5/8 × 22 1/4 inches. Dresden, Staatliche Gemäldegalerie.
101. Miss Lola at the Circus Fernando. 1879. 46 1/16 × 30 5/16 inches. London, Tate Gallery.
102. Carlo Pellegrini, "Ape" of Vanity Fair. Water-colour, with pastel and oil. 24 × 13 inches. London, Tate Gallery.
103. Lady with opera-glass. 18 7/8 × 12 5/8 inches. Dresden, Staatliche Gemäldegalerie.
104. Women ironing. About 1884. 29 15/16 × 32 1/4 inches. Paris, Louvre.
105. Café on the Boulevard Montmartre. Pastel. 1877. 16 1/2 × 23 1/2 inches. Paris, Louvre.

106. Absinthe (Portrait of Hélène Andrée and Marcellin Desboutin, cf. Plate 27). About 1876/77. 36 1/4 × 27 inches. Paris, Louvre.
— (Frontispiece) Prima Ballerina. Pastel. About 1876. 23 × 16 1/2 inches. Paris, Louvre.

HENRI DE TOULOUSE-LAUTREC
(1864-1901)

107. At the Restaurant (Portrait of M. Boileau). 1893. 31 1/2 × 25 1/2 inches. Cleveland, U.S.A., Museum of Art.
108. "Goulue" and her sister at the Moulin Rouge. 1892. 31 1/2 × 23 1/2 inches. Paris, Bernheim Jeune.
109. PORTRAIT. Oil diluted with petrol, on paper. 1893. 26 3/8 × 18 1/2 inches. Paris, Collection Sévadjan.
110. Woman cutting her nails. 1891. 29 1/8 × 25 5/8 inches. London, Mrs. Chester Beatty.
111. A Couple in a drinking-den (À la mie). 1891. 27 1/2 × 19 3/4 inches. Paris, Bernheim Jeune.
112. Portrait of a bearded Gentleman (Portrait of M. de Lauradour). 1897. 32 × 25 1/2 inches. Paris, P. Gallimard.
113. Young Girl in a studio. 1888. Gouache. 29 1/2 × 19 3/4 inches. Bremen, Kunsthalle.
114. Harlot ("Rosa le Rouge"). 1888. 27 1/2 × 18 1/2 inches. Merion, U.S.A., Barnes Foundation.
115. Woman with a black boa. 1892. 20 7/8 × 16 15/16 inches. Paris, Louvre.
116. Miss May Belfort. 1895. 31 1/2 × 23 1/2 inches. Paris, Bernheim Jeune.
117. Promenade at the Moulin Rouge ("La Goulue"). 1891. 31 1/2 × 25 1/2 inches. Paris, Bernheim Jeune.

SOURCES OF PHOTOGRAPHS

Archives Photographiques d'Art et d'Histoire, Paris: 5, 9, 10, 14, 15, 23, 30, 33, 36, 38, 115 ★ Bernheim Jeune, Paris: 80, 84, 85, 108 ★ Braun & Cie., Mulhouse-Dornach: 48, 54, 57 ★ J. E. Bulloz, Paris: 1—4, 8, 11, 13, 16, 18, 25, 31, 32, 40—42, 44, 52, 53, 57, 61, 64, 66, 67, 72, 74, 76, 79, 81, 94, 105, 111, 116 ★ A. C. Cooper, London: 110 ★ M. Durand-Ruel & Cie., Paris: 7, 47, 58, 73, 78, 95 ★ R. B. Fleming & Co., London: 50 ★ Giraudon, Paris: 6, 17, 56, 106 ★ Franz Hanfstaengl, Munich: 20, 60, 65, 87 ★ Morgan, New York: 114 ★ F. Nitzsche, Berlin: 43 ★ Photographische Gesellschaft, Berlin: 55 ★ R. Piper & Co., Munich: 109 ★ Franz Rompel, Hamburg: 28, 29, 39 ★ Anton Schroll & Co., Vienna: 45, 59 ★ Gustav Schwarz, Berlin: 37 ★ Vizzavona, Paris: 19, 24, 27, 88, 107, 112, 117 ★ Museum Photographs: 12, 21, 22, 26, 34, 35, 46, 49, 51, 62, 63, 68—71, 75, 77, 83, 86, 89—93, 98—104, 113.

Drawing by Toulouse-Lautrec